ADVANCE PRAISE FOR

As Sure As Tomorrow Comes

This delightful book is a demonstration of love between a couple who have embraced the true meaning of their wedding vows and notion of God carrying you through. The feelings of happiness, pain, and joy are so real as they experience Romans 8:28: "And we know that all things work together for good to them that love God, to them who are called according to His purpose."

—Karen Bankston, Ph.D., MSN, FACHE, Associate Dean Clinical Practice, Partnership and Community Engagement, Professor Clinical, University of Cincinnati

As Sure As Tomorrow Comes: One Couple's Journey Through Loss and Love is a touching and inspiring book that reveals the power of God in getting through ANY situation. Their willingness and ability to share openly and completely regarding their life's experiences is a testament to their compassion and love for each other and for mankind. Their journey will surely bless others!

—Sonia Jackson Myles, founder, The Sister Accord, LLC, and author, *The Sister Accord: 51 Ways to Love Your Sister*

Chris and Danielle's story is proof that with faith and tenacity, a person can overcome obstacles that life presents them.

—Mary Miller, CEO, Jancoa, and author, *Changing Directions: Ten Choices That Impact Your Dreams*

As Sure As Tomorrow Comes

ONE COUPLE'S JOURNEY THROUGH LOSS AND LOVE

Danielle and Christopher Jones

Cover and book design by Mark Sullivan

ISBN 978-0-9977222-7-7

Georgetown, OH
www.KiCamProjects.com

Printed in the United States of America
Printed on acid-free paper

+ + +

We'd like to dedicate this book to our precious son, Christopher Louis Jones Jr., also known as "Junior." You will forever be your daddy's boy and your mama's baby. We thank God for choosing us to be your parents. Part of our purpose came alive the moment that you came into existence. We will always love you to the moon and back.

In the Book of Ecclesiastes, it's stated that for everything there is a season. The seasons of our lives can take us on some pretty adventurous twists and turns—almost like a roller coaster—whereas other seasons are calm and relaxing.

The funny thing is those seasons don't always correspond with how the weather is outside; they're more about where we are in our lives at a given time. Summer tends to be a lot of fun. Fall is a time of change and transition. Winter is usually cold and bleak, and spring is a time of refreshment, awaiting what is yet to bloom. Life has a way of showing us that no matter what season we've been through, are currently in, or are about to enter, all of them come together to make us who we are.

This is the story of the seasons of our lives so far and how we've remained positive and strong through all kinds of "weather." We pray that our story will encourage you to hold onto hope and faith no matter what season you are in.

Ecclesiastes 3:1-8

For everything there is a season,
a time for every activity under heaven.

A time to be born and a time to die.
A time to plant and a time to harvest.
A time to kill and a time to heal.
A time to tear down and a time to build up.
A time to cry and a time to laugh.
A time to grieve and a time to dance.
A time to scatter stones and a time to gather stones.
A time to embrace and a time to turn away.
A time to search and a time to quit searching.
A time to keep and a time to throw away.
A time to tear and a time to mend.
A time to be quiet and a time to speak.
A time to love and a time to hate.
A time for war and a time for peace.

SUMMER

"Summertime, and the livin' is easy…"
—DuBose Heyward

CHAPTER ONE

As Christopher Jones and I headed into an Italian restaurant, we passed a group of high school girls dressed as though they were enjoying a night on the town before their homecoming dance. The cool November air gently brushed my face as I wore a smile. Chris, the only single man in my age group at our church, had asked me out the week before and now here we were—heading to dinner and a movie for our first date.

Well…depending on which one of us you asked, it was either our first or second date. The week prior, Chris had asked me to hang out with him at an arcade. We went to the arcade and played video games and pool, and since we were enjoying each other's company so much, we ended up going to a nearby mall and walking around and talking. We stayed at the mall almost until it closed. At the end of that night, as he walked me to my car in the mall parking lot, I told Chris I'd had a great time with him. His response was for me not to worry because we'd be seeing each other again—outside of church—real soon. I slyly smirked and drove off.

That very first night of us hanging out, I realized that for the first time since…ever…I felt like I could let my guard down around a man—a potential boyfriend—and just be my goofy self. I was so used to being professional at all times and always crossing every "t" and dotting every "i" that hanging out with Chris was refreshing. He was silly, lighthearted, and made me laugh the entire time we were out.

The days that followed our first evening together were full of Chris and I e-mailing flirtatious messages to each other. It started off with me "being helpful" and offering him some information he could use to write a paper he was working on for one of his college classes. Those messages turned into him asking me to go out with him on another date on the coming Saturday. I had told him repeatedly the time at the arcade and the mall wasn't a date. I mean, sure, he'd asked me to spend time with him. And yes, I'd agreed. And yes, he'd paid for our game of pool. And yes, he had set up the time and place for us to meet. And yes, we were by each other's side the entire night. But I needed him to know that no matter what he thought, that was not a date. He said okay and told me I could call it whatever I wanted to. He just wanted to know if I wanted to go out with him again. And if I did, I needed to be ready for him to pick me up at 6 p.m. Saturday.

So there we were, exactly one week after hanging out at the arcade, heading to dinner and a movie. As we passed by the girls outside the restaurant who were all donning tiaras like princesses, Chris turned to me and asked a question. "Can I crown you my queen one day?" His question completely caught me off guard. He had been flirting with me for six months leading to this night. Over those months, he had thrown just about every pickup line known to man at me, and this whole "crown you my queen one day" line was new and probably one of the best I'd heard. Until then, I'd prided myself on being able to flirt back with clever responses, but I hadn't seen that line coming. It is almost every girl's dream to be some king's queen, and here we were on our first date and this handsome man was asking me to be his. Not knowing how to respond, I stared back at him, laughed a little bit, and (uncharacteristically) shyly said yes. And just like that, I was floating on air for the rest of the night.

About six weeks later, right after our church's New Year's Eve service let out, on January 1 Chris and I solidified our budding relationship. We sat by each other that night at church, and right after the clock struck midnight and people were leaving to go home, we decided we were going to be together. It felt right. It was the start of a new year and it was the start of a new beginning for both of us.

+ + +

For the next three years, we were inseparable. We cared a lot about each other. During this time, I was in grad school until 9:30 p.m. two to three nights a week. Every night I was in school, Chris would drive from his job across town, where he got off at 9 p.m., wait for me to get out of class, and make sure I made it to my car safely. On the nights I wasn't in school, I would make dinner and take it to him so we could have dinner together during the week. On nights when he worked overtime and wouldn't get home until midnight, I would stay up late until he called me to let me know he had made it home okay.

We spent just about every weekend together, and we talked every day. Plus, since we went to the same church, it was a guarantee we'd see each other every Sunday. Neither one of us ever missed a service, and if we ever needed an extra reason to be at church, we'd both found it in each other. We bought bikes and rode together on trails and through neighborhoods. We purchased tennis balls three packs at a time and rackets, even though neither of us knew how to correctly play tennis. We'd find any tennis court we could around town (it didn't matter if it was private or not), and we'd hit our nine balls. Once we'd lost them all, we knew it was time to go. We'd go to arcades and see how many tickets we could win, as if we were little kids. Chris would trade in those tickets for big prizes for me, and I would smile from ear to ear. We'd go to big-box superstores and play hide-and-seek in the aisles. We were happy just being together. I helped him become more serious about his goals, and he helped bring out the silly side of me. We loved each other, and everyone around us knew it.

From the time I was a young teenager, I'd had in my mind the type of man I wanted to marry. I came from a two-parent household, and my parents had gotten married three years before I was born. I believed God would send me someone who I'd have fun with, enjoy life with, and have a family with. Beyond that, I wanted to be with someone who, while dating, could honor the promise I wanted to keep. When I was fourteen years old, I made a promise to myself, God, my parents, and my future husband (whoever he would be) that I wouldn't have sex until I was married. I wanted to save myself for whoever that special person would be. When Chris and I started dating, I made it very clear to him that this was my personal belief and practice and that any man I was going to be in a serious relationship with would have to abide by my desires. Thankfully, Chris said that was fine. He shared with me that he wanted to be celibate, and since I was a virgin, our courtship would be sex-free.

On Halloween, nearly three years after that first date, Chris asked me to come spend some time with him, and I happily obliged. At the time, neither of us was into doing much on Halloween so I figured we'd hang out and watch movies like we'd done so many times before. He was living with his brother and sister-in-law at the time, and they had a newborn baby girl that I was absolutely in love with; I was looking forward to spending time with him and playing with the baby. When I arrived at the house, Chris was doing laundry, his sister-in-law was tending to the baby, and his brother was out of town. Chris met me at the door when I came in. I spoke to his sister-in-law and kissed the baby and followed Chris upstairs to his room. I sat down on his bed and we chatted for a few minutes, and then he left to finish his laundry. He had on a huge T-shirt that was four times too big for him; big, baggy gym shorts; and socks that were pulled up over his calves. To top it off, he had ashy knees that peeked out between the gym shorts and the gym socks. When he returned to the room, he put the basket of clean laundry down and told me he had to ask me something. He grabbed me by the hands, and I stood up. He got down on one knee, looked up at me, and asked, "Will you marry me?"

Chris and I had played around several times with him pretending to ask me to marry him, and I thought this was one of those times. After all, he was doing laundry and his knees looked like he had just played in flour. So I giggled and said, "Yes," like I had so many times before, thinking that surely this was all a joke. But then I caught myself, because when I looked back down at Chris's face and his beautiful brown eyes were staring back at me, I could tell he wasn't joking. He was seriously asking me to be his wife. And I was seriously confused.

I stood there, trying to process what I was feeling. In my mind, when a man proposed, he was supposed to put a great deal of planning and thought into how he was going to do it. And it was okay if he didn't have a ring yet, as long as he asked for a woman's hand in marriage in a special way. Or, if he did have a ring and didn't have some type of grandiose proposal, the ring would more than make up for the lack of atmosphere. But there we stood, in Chris's bedroom, without a ring and without a fantasy-like proposal. And

I didn't know what to do. This was the man who over the course of three years had stolen my heart. He'd brought teddy bears and cards to my job. He would even send surprise candy and fruit basket deliveries to me. All of my coworkers were telling us he was going to get the boyfriend/husband of the year award for being so sweet to me. Surely this wasn't my knight in shining armor's idea of a great proposal! What the heck was really going on? But sure enough, on the night that my heartthrob of a man proposed, he did it in gym socks, gym shorts, and a T-shirt and had no ring.

"You will? You'll marry me?" He smiled back at me excitedly as I shook myself back to reality. He was excited and I was…trying to figure out what had happened. "Yes! Yes, I'll marry you!" I said with a big smile on my face but confusion in my brain.

He got up, gave me a kiss, and ran downstairs to tell his sister-in-law our good news.

When I went downstairs, his sister-in-law gave me a huge hug and said congratulations. I asked her if she'd known Chris was going to ask me to marry him that night, and she said he'd mentioned it to her. I gave her a *look*—one of those piercing looks that she could feel. I felt like she had just broken one of the unspoken girl code rules.

Rule: No woman will ever let another woman's man propose to her in a bootleg way.

How could she let him ask me to marry him without telling him to at least pick up flowers or candy or hell, even a card?! But she'd just had a baby six weeks prior and she said that her "girl code radar" was down at the moment and she was sorry I was feeling disappointed. She told me she was just excited that we weren't going to follow the world's standards of how everything was done and that she was happy for us. *Yeah, yeah, yeah,* I thought. She hadn't just been proposed to by a man in gym socks and shorts without a ring.

Looking back on it, I was being vain, and there is nothing good about being vain. But in the moment—one of the biggest moments in either of our lives—I wanted to stand there and be amazed at how my future husband asked me to marry him. And instead of being amazed, I was disappointed. So, after we went back upstairs, I did what any vain girl would've done: I asked him if he could ask me to marry him again the next day. He looked at me and got mad. "Why do I need to do that?" he asked. I responded with my truth: "Because I want to have a story to tell!" He looked at me and stormed out of the room. I was sad because my man hadn't granted me my dream proposal, and he was sad because his girlfriend was disappointed. On that night, we were probably the two saddest newly engaged people in history.

Over the next few weeks, Chris told me he was sorry I wasn't too thrilled about the way he'd asked me to marry him. He'd just wanted to know if I'd be his wife. He had worked up the nerve to ask me and hadn't really put a whole lot of thought into how he was going to do it. Plus, when he asked, he didn't really have the money to buy me a ring. He was simply trying to get the question out. I felt bad after he shared his thoughts with me. Chris was sincere and he had been nothing but a sweetheart to me during our courtship. He'd been full of nerves trying to ask me to marry him, and I was looking for fairy dust and unicorns to fall out of the sky so I'd have some amazing proposal story to share. He kept on telling me that if I gave him a chance, he'd make it up to me when he presented me with my ring. I believed him. After all, this was the guy who made me laugh every day, who brightened my world with so much joy, and who let me know that true love existed. So, I settled it within myself that he had something up his sleeve, and I waited patiently to see how everything would unfold. Grand proposal or not, we were engaged, and I was going to be with the man I loved forever.

+ + +

Six weeks after the initial proposal, Chris told me he wanted to take me out to dinner. He suggested that I wear something nice, and of course I obliged. On December 12, he picked me up from my house and we drove back to the Italian restaurant where we'd had our first date. When we walked in, I was surprised to see several of our family members, my best friend, and two of our other close friends. I had an inkling that something special was in the works for us that night.

The host sat our party in the same place where Chris and I had had our first date. In the middle of dinner, Chris stood up and said he had an announcement to make. He shared with our family and friends how on our first date we'd passed the girls with the tiaras. He told everyone about his "queen" question and, looking at me, he told me to tell everyone what my response had been. Through laughter, I told them how I'd said yes, he could crown me his queen one day. After I said it, he pulled out a paper crown and placed it on my head. Next, he got down on one knee, pulled out a ring box, and asked me to marry him. I shouted yes, and when he popped the ring box open, there was a ring he had made from bread ties! He made me show off my bread-tie ring to everyone, and we were all laughing. He then pulled out another box from his pocket, opened it, and asked me if I would marry him. The ring was the most beautiful ring I'd ever seen. I shrieked, while almost crying out of joy, and said yes. Chris and I hugged and kissed each other. Afterward, there were several cheers and claps from our family and friends and other diners. The manager immediately brought out glasses and a bottle of champagne. That proposal came from the man I knew.

After dinner was over and our family and friends had left, Chris turned to me and said, "Now you've got your story to tell." And I looked back at him and said, "I sure do!"

+ + +

A year and a half later, in May 2011, our wedding ceremony was beautiful, and our five-day honeymoon cruise the following week was awesome. There were moments when I thought I'd cry tears of joy from being so happy. My face was frozen in a smile the entire time. I had kept my promise to God of not having sex until after I was married, I was marrying the love of my life, and I was sure that our life together would be wonderful. We were entering into pure bliss with a strong network of family, friends, coworkers, and church family who supported us and loved us. And if I needed any more goodness to happen, one week after we returned from our honeymoon, I participated in my graduate degree ceremony, having earned my MBA three months prior. Life was looking good for us, and I was loving it.

FALL

"In every change, in every falling leaf, there is some pain, some beauty, and that's the way new leaves grow."

—Amit Ray

CHAPTER TWO

Nine months after getting married, Chris shared with me that he had been contemplating switching jobs. He'd been working at the same company for the last ten years and he was ready to do something different. He wanted to broaden his horizons and grow his skill set. He also wanted the opportunity to make more money. I fully supported him in his endeavors. He'd found a logistics company he wanted to work for, and it seemed like a good fit. The work atmosphere was great and he'd be challenged to grow in a few areas where he wanted to gain more experience. There was a heavy focus on sales, which he had never really done much of, but he was confident he could rise to the challenge and excel. For the first couple of months, he came home happy every day. It did my heart good to see my husband energized by his work. He felt good about his job, and he showed it—in the office and at home. He mentioned that there was a quota he would have to reach by the end of his sixth month or he'd lose his job, but neither he nor I was worried about it. Chris was a hard worker who wanted to make sure he performed well at his job so he could bring more money into our household. He took being a financial contributor and provider seriously, and he never wanted us to struggle.

I never could've seen it coming, but in the midst of the transition to the new job, Chris shared with me that there was another transition he was contemplating for us. One day, while we were riding in the car together, he turned to me and said, "I think God is leading us to leave our church."

His statement completely caught me off guard. Chris had been a member of our church for more than ten years, and I had been there for almost six. About a month before we got married, Chris had been named a minister, and for the last two years I had been going though intense deaconate training with several other members. We'd met at our church, we'd grown spiritually there, and we were there every weekend either involved in some church activity or for worship service. We were also there once during the week for Bible study. Both of us were involved in various ministries, and we had developed strong bonds with the people with whom we worshipped on a regular basis. Our church members had become like family to both of us.

"How do you feel about that?" he asked me as I started to think about what he had just said.

"Well," I replied, "if that's what you feel like God is leading us to do, then I'm for it. I'll just miss the people." My love for the people was incredible. I had grown especially close to the liturgical dancers. There were so many of us, and we loved each other. We saw each other at church on Sundays and checked in on each other during the week. I was going to miss my church girlfriends, but I resolved within myself that if our bonds were truly as strong as I thought they were, they would survive me being at another church.

"So, where do you want us to go to church from now on?" I asked him. We were too involved not to be members of any church, and I knew that fellowshipping with other Christians was important to both of us. "I'm not sure yet, but I'm thinking we'll try one of the newer churches that has recently moved into town," he said.

"Well, if you think that's what we're supposed to do, then let's go for it." I wasn't quite sure what would be next on our church journey, but I did know I was trying my hardest to be a wife who listened to her husband and took his lead.

+ + +

By the fifth month of Chris working at his new job, he still hadn't met the sales quota he'd need to reach by the end of his sixth month, and though he was a little concerned about it, he remained confident he'd reach it. The office stayed open twenty-four hours a day; it was a company that operated in every time zone across the United States, so sometimes it was necessary for people to work odd hours. Because Chris hadn't yet reached his quota, I encouraged him to stay at the office a few extra hours every night, but he decided against it. He told me we were a newly married couple and he didn't want work to get in the way of us enjoying each other's company. I'd made it a practice to not check work e-mails or to focus on work-related projects after hours (as much as I could), and he had done the same thing.

In August 2012, the sixth month of Chris being at his new company, my family and Chris and I went on vacation with our vacation club. We stayed at a beautiful five-star, all-inclusive resort in the Caribbean and experienced all sorts of fun. We swam in an underwater cave, we went zip-lining through the jungle, we had only the best fine-dining experiences, and we relaxed at the spa. All of us agreed it was the best family vacation we'd ever taken. But during the vacation, Chris seemed a little anxious about his job. He'd brought his work computer with him and he was constantly keeping up with everything that was happening back in his office. He had just closed one deal for the company, which put him closer to reaching his quota—but it still wasn't enough to put him over the top. After we returned from vacation, he'd only have a few days to meet his sales mark or he'd lose his job.

After getting home on Saturday, Chris returned to work Monday, determined to meet his quota. On his way home from work that Wednesday, he called me with the news he didn't want to share: "Babe, I lost my job."

I had been lying across the bed watching a game show, but with those words, everything stopped. I sat up. "O-o-okay," I said slowly.

"They said that I'd done a really great job but they still had to let me go because I didn't meet the quota," Chris said.

"Well, that's okay," I reassured him. "That's not a problem at all. It'll be okay, and we'll be okay."

Chris previously had worked at the same place for ten years without any problems, so surely he would be able to find another job quickly. He had an associate's degree in business and almost had enough credits to get an associate's degree in finance. He had a bachelor's degree in marketing, and at the job prior to the one he had just lost, he had been an assistant supervisor. The loss of this job would just be a small test we would get past. Didn't all married couples go through some sort of trial? I saw him losing his job as our first real adventure in being married. We'd be just fine.

When Chris switched from his long-standing job to go to the logistics company, he'd taken a pay cut of a few hundred dollars per paycheck every two weeks. Though we knew what our monthly expenses would be, we never adjusted them to reconcile what was going out against what we now had coming in. We kept believing that Chris was going to hit the quota at his job and get a pay increase, which would've put us back to what he originally was earning. Thankfully, a few weeks after losing his job, Chris learned he would be eligible for unemployment benefits, which would be a great help to us. However, it wasn't what he had made at either job he'd had previously. But it was something, and for us, that would work.

We still had bills, though…and bills don't care if you have enough money to pay them or not—they show up as sure as tomorrow comes. And when you don't have a job to pay those bills, they seem to come even faster—rent, food, car note, car insurance, gas for the cars, life insurance, renter's insurance, utilities, plus other everyday living expenses. Because we had bills and no money to pay them, we used a credit card to help.

In the days after Chris lost his job, he updated his résumé, spoke with a career coach, and applied for several jobs. Those days turned into weeks, which turned into months, and he still hadn't gotten any job offers. He was at home every day while I was at work. He was trying to find ways to stay occupied during the day, but nothing was as fulfilling to him as a job would've been.

One day I came home and Chris was sitting in the dark in our living room. It made me sad to see him like that. In all the years I'd known him, I'd never seen him so down. He was always so jovial and full of life. And on this day, it felt like my husband had started to lose hope. I sat on the couch next to him, took his hand, and told him it would all be okay. We had each other to get through the tough times. He shared with me that he'd never wanted to be married without a job. He took his responsibility as a husband seriously and he wanted so badly to take care of our home. That day I just listened to his heart. I was married to a man who loved me more than anyone had ever loved me before. He wanted to take care of me and take care of us. He was a manly man who prided himself on going to work every day and making a good living. And losing his job took that away from him. I assured him we would be fine. We'd always lived by the principle that God was our provider, not us. And since He had us in this situation, He would continue to provide for us. Our principles and beliefs were being tested, and we were staring them down. Either we were going to believe what we'd always claimed we believed, or we were going to falter at this sign of trouble.

Over the next few weeks, Chris shared with me that he didn't want to just sit at home all day with nothing to do, and since he hadn't yet gotten many job interviews, he decided to enroll in a few online photography classes. Photography was something he'd recently gotten interested in, and I was happy he'd found something to do that could make him happy. He ended up finding a few in-person classes near our home that he decided to take, as well. He enjoyed going to the classes, and I enjoyed hearing about them. I got to be his model for his practice sessions, and he got a kick out of teaching me all of the cool stuff he was learning. We were still praying for him to get a job, but the photography classes gave us both something to look forward to.

In the meantime, as Chris had planned, we decided to start going to a church that was new to town. Chris liked the preacher's style, and the preacher's messages helped Chris discover how much love God has for him. But for me, I didn't feel like I was getting the sense of community that we had been so used to at our other church. There was only one other couple at the new church that was in our age range, and though we enjoyed seeing them each week, I still felt like something was missing. I wanted so badly to attend with my husband, but I just didn't feel all the way "home" there. The church streamed its services, so for a variety of reasons, we stopped attending church in person and started watching it online. This gave us the opportunity to tune in to church together from the comfort of home.

+ + +

In April 2013, Chris and I were at home. I was upstairs in our bedroom and he was downstairs in the living room. All of a sudden, he started screaming my name. I immediately ran down the stairs to find Chris on the floor, grabbing one side of his body. Scared, I helped him get up and get situated on the couch. I asked him if he was okay and to tell me what happened.

His brother and sister-in-law now had two little girls. The youngest was about eight months old and was learning how to crawl. She couldn't quite figure out how to fully maneuver both of her legs at the same time, and Chris would always chuckle when he saw her do it. Goofing around and being silly, he decided he'd try to imitate her. As he was doing that, his right leg had gone numb, which caused him to drop to the floor, and that's when he yelled for me to come help him.

At first, I tried to figure out why Chris's right leg would go numb. Maybe his blood wasn't circulating properly. Or maybe he'd been sitting so long on the couch that by the time he'd gotten down on the floor, his leg had just given out on him. Or maybe—I didn't want to dwell on the thought too long, but I at least considered it—maybe these were the first signs of something more serious.

In my teens and early twenties, I'd become increasingly interested in health and how the body works. As I finished my undergraduate college years, I struggled within because I wanted to tie my business acumen with my passion for people and the things that mattered to people, but I wasn't sure how God would bring it all together. Thankfully, within six months of graduating with my public relations degree, it was as if God had created the perfect job for me: a media relations position at a children's hospital. It was my dream job. I'd be able to put my PR knowledge to work while also enhancing my knowledge of health care. In addition to that, I could be around children and their families, which I absolutely loved. So on the day my husband fell and told me one side of his body was numb, I quickly ran through my repertoire of illnesses, and multiple sclerosis was the one my inner dial landed on.

To that point, I'd known only one other young person who had been diagnosed with MS. A friend's husband had been diagnosed five years prior. Like us, they were in their early thirties; he'd been diagnosed one month before they got married. Health-wise, they seemed to be doing extremely well, but the thought of MS still made me a little scared of what the outcomes were.

While sitting on the couch that day, I asked Chris a variety of questions. Had he ever felt any numbness or tingling anywhere else in his body? If he was or had been hurt, he'd never tell me unless I pried for information. Plus, according to him, my most annoying trait was me asking way too many questions about everything. In spite of his annoyance with me, he shared that recently he'd been noticing some tingling in his right arm and that it had been falling asleep a lot. Initially he and I thought maybe his arm was falling asleep because of him playing a video game on his phone during the day as he waited for companies to call him back for job interviews. Just to be sure nothing serious was happening, I encouraged him to call the doctor the next morning.

About a week later, a primary care physician told Chris it was no big deal and that we were right: His arm tingling and falling asleep was probably due to him playing the game on his phone. The doctor suggested that Chris lay off the game for a while. We were relieved, and Chris decided to put the phone down and focus more on his photography classes.

But a week later, Chris starting having muscle spasms. The entire right side of his body would contort and curl up. Each time, his torso would bend over and he would look like the letter "C." These episodes would last for about twenty seconds each. They were very scary. Chris's hand would automatically ball up into a fist, his face would get stuck in an expression that seemed like he was in pain, he wouldn't be able to talk, and the entire right side of his body would be stiff. Neither of us had ever seen anything like it, and we were concerned. The spasms would come and go, and we never knew when another one would happen or why they were happening, so Chris made another appointment with his primary care physician. The doctor now knew that this was more than just a simple case, but he still couldn't quite diagnose Chris with any specific medical condition.

Over the next couple of weeks, Chris was still having the muscle spasms and we couldn't figure out why. Sometimes they would come along with heavy sweating. And sometimes one side of Chris's body would go numb. We weren't sure what was going on, but we kept on praying and believing that all would be fine. The spasms were inconsistent. Sometimes they'd come two to three times a day, and sometimes they wouldn't come at all. Sometimes they'd come in the middle of the night, and sometimes they'd come early in the morning. Chris said he never really knew when they were going to come. Each time one happened, he'd get a tingling feeling in his leg about five seconds before his entire body would tighten up. Each time the tingling would start, he knew he'd have to hold onto something very quickly and brace himself for what was to come.

Even with the mysterious muscle spasms, we were still trying to live our lives as normally as possible. At the time, Chris was still looking for a full-time job, and though he was in good spirits, he had started to get a little discouraged about his search. It was time for a getaway. Both of our birthdays are in May, and Chris knew the only thing I really wanted for my birthday was to go out of town.

Though money was a little tight, Chris really wanted to make my wish come true. For his thirtieth birthday, the year prior, I'd thrown him a surprise birthday party dinner with our family and friends. So for my thirtieth birthday, he had a surprise up his sleeve for me, too. In the days leading up to my birthday, Chris told me to pack a suitcase because we were going out of town. I had no idea where we were going, and he wasn't giving me any clues until we got on the road and started driving. He had saved some money and had found a great deal to make my only birthday wish come true. When we were about an hour from our home, he told me he'd made reservations for five days and four nights at a luxurious, indoor, all-inclusive resort in Tennessee that we'd walked through earlier in the year while I was at a conference. We'd always talked about returning as guests, and I couldn't have been more excited. He was proud of himself for planning our trip without help from anyone, and I was proud to be married to my thoughtful husband.

During our first days at the resort, we did nothing but walk around and take in the beauty of everything. Our room had a balcony, which became my favorite part about the room. Each morning we could look down on the palm trees and stone-paved walkways that ran through the common areas. We purposely didn't wear watches or keep up with the time, because we were truly enjoying the peacefulness of being on vacation and it just being the two of us. It was like a second honeymoon. Just Chris and me, together and in love. It was the best birthday present ever. Once again, my favorite guy in the whole world had managed to put a never-ending smile on my face.

On the third day of our trip, we decided to visit a nearby outlet mall. We went into any store that appealed to us, but since we were trying not to spend a ton of money, we did a lot of window shopping.

However, Chris took me into one of my favorite clothing stores and told me to pick out a dress I really liked and it would be part of my birthday present. Even though I hesitated, he insisted. He really enjoyed buying clothes for me, and even though he was between jobs, he took great pride in setting aside a bit of money to do so. And, to my surprise, he also was really good at picking out clothes for me! Chris did it better than I did for myself. We had each other's tastes nailed down to a tee. I'd pick out dapper ties and cuff links for him, and he always knew what would look good on me. That day, Chris and I each picked out a new dress for me for my birthday.

As we were headed out of the store with our purchases, Chris quickly grabbed one of the clothing racks just before a twenty-second muscle spasm came on. The sales associates came over to check on him, but he told them he was fine. I was scared for my husband and didn't know what to do other than to pray and suggest that he call the doctor. He wasn't quite sold on calling the doctor yet.

After leaving the mall, I suggested we get a heating pad to see if that would help calm or stop the spasms. On the way to the store, we saw a bowling alley and decided we'd go bowling after picking up the heating pad.

At the bowling alley, we made it only to the fourth frame of the game before Chris had another spasm. It came on fast and caused him to lean over, once again making the "C" shape. As onlookers stared, trying to figure out what was happening, I felt bad for my husband. These spasms seemed to be coming more frequently, and we didn't know why or what to do about them. After recovering from the spasm, Chris sat down and turned to me and said he was ready to leave. Back at the resort, we plugged in the heating pad and applied it to his back, but as quickly as we applied it, he had another spasm.

On the fourth day of our vacation, we decided to venture into the city's downtown area. We walked around and took in the sights.

Chris brought his camera and took pictures of everything he saw. He was eager to put some of his newfound camera skills to work, and I enjoyed pointing out places and things for him to take pictures of.

After taking a horse-drawn carriage ride around town, we decided to get ice cream. We both ordered two scoops of ice cream on waffle cones and headed back outside into the Tennessee summer heat. As soon as we got outside, Chris suddenly told me to take his ice cream from him. I grabbed it out of his hand while he put his other hand against the brick wall of the ice cream shop just before a spasm began. I stood there and watched him, not knowing what to do but to ask him, "Are you okay, honey? Are you okay?" He did the best he could to nod yes, and after the spasm was over, he stood back up straight, took a deep breath and slowly took his ice cream back from me.

In that moment, I was more scared for my husband's health than I ever had been before.

We walked slowly back to the car, hand in hand. I wanted my husband to know that no matter what these spasms meant, I loved him and would be by his side. That night, I again suggested he call his doctor and tell him what had happened on our trip.

As we pulled back into the resort parking lot, Chris was on the phone with the doctor and I heard him say, "Aw, man!" He later told me that the doctor still didn't know what was causing the spasms, but that they were serious enough that Chris shouldn't drive over the next few days. He also referred him to a neurologist.

Before that night was over, Chris had a total of eight debilitating spasms, and nothing seemed to calm them down. It was the most he'd ever had in one day. The next morning, we left town, not knowing what the days ahead would hold.

CHAPTER THREE

Two days after we returned home, Chris took his mom's advice and went to see a neurologist. Chris told the doctor about all of the tingling, numbness, and spasms, and I shared video I'd taken of Chris's spasms in Tennessee. I knew that once we were able to get to a doctor, the video might prove helpful. The neurologist asked Chris a series of questions and viewed the videos I'd taken. The doctor wasn't sure what to make of the symptoms, so he referred Chris to a nurse practitioner, and in the meantime, Chris's primary care physician ordered tests.

By the end of August, Chris had gone through a spinal tap, two MRIs, an EEG, an EKG, and a CT scan and had had more than a hundred vials of blood drawn from him. We were at the hospital with Chris getting tests just about every week. The doctors didn't know what was wrong, the spasms were still happening, and we'd felt like we'd had one of the worst summers ever.

The one highlight for me was finding another church that I absolutely loved. My godmother had been telling me about it. Chris and I had visited it once, and although it wasn't quite Chris's style, I had fallen in love with it. They were focused on outreach and meeting the needs of the people in the community, and I loved that. Plus, there were a lot of young couples just like Chris and me. If there were ever a church that I wanted to be a part of, it was this one. Before even joining, I had gotten involved in their outreach ministry. While Chris preferred good old biblical teaching of the Word of God, I enjoyed the entire church experience, with the worship music, the preached Word, and seeing all the people. Chris and I realized that what each of us wanted and needed out of a church were two different things, and while I didn't knock him for still wanting to go to the other church, he didn't knock me for going to the church I liked. We both still loved God and His Word. We both still had a strong relationship and connection with Him individually and collectively, but what we needed and wanted out of a local worshiping body were two completely different things.

Chris was still keeping his eyes open for any sign of a good-paying full-time job. By this time, a year had passed without him working full time. In addition to working at the townhome/apartment complex, he was still getting an unemployment check, but it wasn't enough for us to cover all of our bills. We decided to take some advice we'd once heard. We would pay the most important bills, but others would need to wait. We knew we had used the credit card to purchase some items. Before Chris lost his job, we had always paid the credit card bill so as not to accrue any late fees. But with money getting tighter and tighter and Chris' medical bills starting to add up, we decided to stop making payments on the credit card so we could use that money for other bills that we had to pay. In deciding to stop paying on it, we also decided to stop using it. At that point, we'd accumulated about $4,500 in debt on the card. We knew we'd pay it back one day, but at that point in time, we needed the money to pay for food and electricity.

+ + +

After all of the medical tests, doctor visits, bills, blood draws, and speculation over what could possibly be going on in Chris's body, we finally got our answer in November 2013. Chris went to see the neurology nurse practitioner, who told him that all the test results and her own medical knowledge indicated a diagnosis of MS. The most recent MRI and CT scans showed that Chris had four lesions, or scarring, on his brain and spine. Those lesions were causing the tingling, the numbness, and those terrible spasms.

We didn't know much about MS, but based on what we did know, getting an MS diagnosis wasn't good. Chris's first words were, "I'm not going to let this thing get to me. I'm going to be just fine." I agreed with him and told him I was glad that at least we had a diagnosis so we could figure out what to do to help him.

Within a week of the diagnosis, a nurse came to our house and showed Chris how to use a self-injecting medication. He'd have to give himself shots three to four days a week to reduce his flare-ups.

Over time, the medication seemed to be working with no side effects, and Chris was doing a great job of fighting MS. Both of us kept positive attitudes and were confident that Chris would be okay. In fact, Chris's positive attitude about the diagnosis and his determination to live through it helped calm my nerves. If he wasn't going to be worried about it, then I wasn't either.

+ + +

My mother is a breast cancer survivor who was diagnosed at the age of thirty-seven. Because of that, doctors wanted to watch my breast health very closely. Whereas most women start getting mammograms once a year at the age of forty, I had to start getting them ten years prior to the age my mother was when she was diagnosed, so for me, that meant twenty-seven.

In October, I knew I needed to have my mammogram, but for some reason, I kept pushing my appointment back. Then, one day as I was watching my favorite morning show, one of the anchors announced that doctors had discovered she had breast cancer when she had gotten a mammogram as part of one of the show's news stories. This particular reporter had volunteered to get a mammogram on live TV to show viewers there was nothing scary about getting tested for breast cancer. Only a short time later, the reporter went back on the show to reveal that doctors had found stage II breast cancer. Her story made me pick up the phone immediately and schedule my mammogram.

When I went for my appointment, the doctor scanned both of my breasts, left the room, and came back. She said she was concerned about two spots she'd located. I didn't know what she meant, but I didn't like that she'd found anything. She told me she wanted me to come back and get a breast biopsy so she could check the spots more carefully.

One week later, and two weeks after my husband was diagnosed with MS, I lay still on the exam table while the doctors stuck a needle into my breast in two different locations and extracted fluid from the "spots" they'd seen. As I lay on the table, tears rolled down my face. The anesthetic and the needle the doctors used burned more than the extraction did. I didn't know if the tears were from the stinging of the first needle they used to numb me, the thought of the second needle they were using to do the actual biopsy, the fact that my husband had just been diagnosed with MS, the fact that our financial situation was tight, or that life just did not feel good at the time.

I tried to joke with the nurses about how my husband said my breasts were causing issues and that because of that he called them "belligerent titties." They chuckled and so did I, but as I lay there, hot tears rolled down my face as I tightly squeezed a stress relief ball with one hand and a nurse's hand with the other. This whole experience sucked. My husband had just been diagnosed with a chronic illness and here I was with my "belligerent titties" lying on a darn gurney in a room that was super small and cold. How in the world did I end up here?

I had brought Chris to the appointment with me, hoping he could come back to the room with me when the biopsy happened, but due to hospital policy, he had to stay in the waiting room. I wish he could've been with me. He always made me—and everyone else around us—laugh. He had a very straightforward yet comedic way of putting things into perspective, and I appreciated that about him. After my appointment, he walked me to the car and helped me crawl into bed when I got home. He brought me chicken soup and made sure I was comfortable that night.

The following week, we got the results back, and neither spot was cancerous. They were benign lesions called fibroadenomas that didn't cause cancer but that the doctors wanted to watch closely. That week, on Thanksgiving Day, we had a lot to be thankful for. Things might not have been perfect, but God was good. We were alive, we were well, and we were grateful to have our family and friends.

CHAPTER FOUR

In February 2014, Chris got the call he had been waiting for. He was being hired at a national bank that had several local branches. He'd been able to take some photos of our families and friends during the holiday season, and things were looking up for us. Finally, things were starting to get back on track, and that felt good.

Chris was excited to be working again and I was excited for him. During his first two weeks of work, he would come home and have me quiz him on bank terms he needed to know to be successful at his job. We would sit up in our bed at night with flash cards spread across the bed, and he would tell me the answers forward and backward. He knew his stuff and I was proud of him. And he was proud of himself.

We were sure Chris would excel at the bank. He was always a math whiz. In middle school and high school, he focused on math as a way to stay out of trouble—especially since getting in trouble was easy for him, being that he was his classmates' favorite jokester. Math came easy to him; when others had to use a calculator, Chris could work out problems and have the right answer in his head. Before we got married, he'd started a math tutoring business and helped students go from earning failing grades and barely getting by to earning A's and B's and being proud of themselves. If anyone could work at a bank, surely it was Chris.

As for me, I soon learned I'd be getting a promotion. I'd be making more money and I'd have more responsibility. When I learned about the promotion, I felt awesome. My husband was doing well in his job, and things were starting to turn the corner for us.

I could finally breathe a little and settle into this life of me being happy, my husband being happy, and us getting ahead.

CHAPTER FIVE

I'm a family girl through and through. My great-grandmother on my father's side was one of eleven children, and my great grandmother on my mother's side was one of sixteen children. Our family believes in and practices loving each other no matter how distant relatives we may be. In fact, I'm very close to some of my second and third cousins, and we all love it that way.

I was blessed as a child, a young adult, and even now, as a young woman, to have my mom's parents and grandparents and my dad's mother and grandmother in my life. My parents worked hard to make sure that my brother and I had a close relationship with our elders, and I appreciate the extra effort they put in to make sure we knew and spent time with the matriarchs and patriarchs of our family.

My great-uncle, my grandfather's brother on my mom's side, owned a huge dairy farm about three hours south of where we lived. I will always remember when my immediate family, my grandparents, and great-grandparents traveled down to the farm when I was about fifteen years old for our family reunion. I remember that while it was completely foreign to me, I was amused with farm life. When I visited, I was the typical city-girl teenager who loved shopping, talking on the phone, and going to movies. But when I was on the farm, I learned all about waking up early to milk cows and how even if a person's closest neighbor is a mile away, they still have a tight-knit community.

By 2014, it had been sixteen years since our family had gone down to the farm and since many of us had seen one another. We all still talked so fondly of one another and knew that one day we'd see each other again. On June 1, that day came. As it turned out, my great uncle, aunt, two of their twelve kids, and four of their grandkids would be driving through Cincinnati on their way back from a loved one's funeral. Since they hadn't seen my grandfather or several of us since the farm visit, they'd talked with my mom about stopping through the city on their way back to Kentucky; that way, my grandfather could spend time with his brother and all of us could hang out and catch up. My mom, the hostess who does the mostest, was all for a family visit.

My grandfather talked more during his brother's visit than I'd ever heard him talk before. It was as if this was one of the best nights of his life. The ironic thing was my great-uncle hadn't been all that keen on making the trip. But my great-uncle's children talked him into going to the funeral for his wife's family member, which is what brought them through Cincinnati; my grandfather, who could be a little choosy about where he decided to go and not go, was eager to come visit with everyone that night. It was as if the stars aligned and this family visit was destined to happen.

That night my grandfather shared stories with all of us, and we laughed the whole night. He told us about his childhood and how he and his siblings used to get into mischief that only they could have gotten into while growing up in the 1930s and late 1940s. And his brother, my great-uncle who is seven years older, added to the stories. They talked about their parents and about their aunts and uncles. My grandfather shared stories about serving in the Korean War; he even shared the story about how when he first saw my grandmother, he thought she was the prettiest woman he'd ever seen.

When it started getting dark outside on my parents' deck, we all moved inside and the laughs continued for the rest of the night. It was the crickets, my parents' patio light, and the sounds of our laughing at my granddaddy and his brother that lit up the night and made it come alive.

Before my great-uncle, great aunt, and extended family got back on the road, we all took pictures together and vowed to visit with each other soon. My cousins and I all got connected on social media that night, and our love and appreciation for the bond between our elders and their history grew.

Two weeks later, it was Father's Day, and as usual, I visited my parents' church to spend the day with my dad and mom. After the church service and dinner, my parents, Chris, myself, and my brother visited my grandparents' house to wish my granddad a happy Father's Day.

When we pulled up, I found him in one of his usual spots, sitting at the side of the house on top of a homemade seat he had created out of a tree stump. "Howdy!" he said, smiling, as we all got out of our cars. My granddaddy was one of the most unique people I knew. Ever since I was a little girl, his greeting was "Howdy!" I didn't know anyone else who said it, but I learned from an early age that that was granddaddy's way of saying hello. I greeted him back with a laugh, "Howdy to you too, Granddaddy! Happy Father's Day!" I gave him a hug and a kiss and handed him a card with a gift card inside. Granddaddy wasn't too hard to shop for. He shopped at the same grocery store every time, and although he loved coffee, there were two restaurants in particular that he got coffee from. The card I handed him was accompanied with a gift card for him to get coffee, and I was sure he'd enjoy his Father's Day gift. We all went inside to say hello to my grandmother, while my grandfather enjoyed the warm summer day.

As we were all leaving, I told Granddaddy I'd had so much fun spending time with him and my great aunt and uncle just two weeks earlier. He smiled and agreed and chuckled. *Yep, that's Granddaddy,* I thought. As I was getting ready to walk back to my car, my dad said in a playful tone, "Go on over there and hop in a picture with Granddaddy!" I obliged and kneeled down next to the tree stump that my grandfather was sitting on and smiled through a laugh.

Granddaddy was so funny to me. He was the only person I knew of who would actually cut a stump from a tree and sit on it. He spent his days tinkering with all types of little things around the house. In his later years, he had developed an affection for birds and bird feeders. He would read up on what type of feed to purchase to attract certain kinds of birds. He'd always been a big fan of all types of cars, and he enjoyed sharing his knowledge of how cars and car parts worked. When I was in high school, he taught me how to give my own car an oil change and how to change a flat tire. For years, he'd owned his own upholstering business, and he could build and fix anything. From banisters to armoires, to chairs, desks, bedframes, doors...there was nothing he couldn't build or fix. And he always found something to do in the yard. Whether he was whacking the bushes or cutting the grass, he seemed to like being outside and experiencing what Mother Nature had to offer. He would start his morning when the sun went up with his cup of coffee and working in his shop at the end of his driveway. And at the end of the night, he could be found in front of the television in the living room dozing off with my grandma gently nudging him, telling him it was time for them to retreat to their room upstairs.

Granddaddy never called anyone by their first name. You just kind of knew he was talking to you when he looked in your direction and said "Howdy!" In fact, I remember my granddaddy calling me by my first name only one time, and that was when we went to the family farm for the family reunion when I was fifteen. But that didn't matter, because he was Granddaddy. Granddaddy had a special love for all of his grandkids, and we loved him back. He took all of us fishing, he played with us, he shared funny stories with us, and he always urged us to ask Grandma for snacks. He took us bike riding and fishing, and all nine grandkids knew we could get away with just about anything when we were with Granddaddy! He was our buddy, and we were his.

When my daddy told me to get next to Granddaddy on Father's Day so we could take a picture, I had no idea it would be the last time I saw my buddy, my granddaddy, and one of my superheroes.

Ten days after Father's Day, I was getting dressed for work when my phone rang. It was right around 8 a.m. and I was rushing to get out of the door, but I answered the call because it was my father. He said to me calmly, "Baby girl, you may want to sit down. Granddaddy died this morning." My world stopped, and I didn't know what to do. I stared at myself in the mirror and couldn't believe the words I was hearing. "What happened?" My dad said that they weren't sure yet but they believed my grandfather had suffered a heart attack. I told my dad that I would go over to my grandparents' house immediately and I hung up the phone.

Driving to my grandparents' house, I couldn't believe what had happened. I'd just seen my granddad ten days prior—sitting on his stump, at the bottom of my grandparents' steps that led to their back door that we all used to get into the house. And before that, I'd seen him fifteen days prior, laughing on my parents' deck and patio, talking about his childhood and his war days. I didn't understand how this could be happening. Or why.

When I got to my grandparents' house, my mom, her parents' youngest child, was the first to hug me. Her mom seemed to be calm but in a state of semi-shock. We were all trying to figure out how the easygoing, non-stressed man had died. My mom explained to all of us that my grandmother had called her that morning right around seven o'clock and told my mom that my grandfather was cold and he wasn't moving. My mom told her to immediately call 911 and that she'd be there as quickly as possible. When my mother arrived, there were a fire truck, a police car, and an ambulance already at my grandparents' house. My mom spoke with the paramedics and explained the situation and who was inside. She asked them if my granddad was okay, and they gently told her he had passed away.

On that day, June 26, 2014, a small piece of my heart broke. My great-grandparents, whom I had also been close to, had passed away when I was in my twenties, and although many of my friends knew what it was like to lose one or both grandparents, I hadn't experienced that yet. The situation was magnified because we'd just been with my grandfather. It was almost eerie, because it was as if he knew his days on earth were coming to an end and he made the decision to live out those final days by spending them with his family.

Granddaddy may have been a quiet man, but he was loud when it came to the love he showed his family. Even on the day he passed away, there was food in the refrigerator he had cooked only the day before, which we were able to eat. That was Granddaddy. He did what he needed to do to make sure his family was taken care of.

Over the next several days, family and friends came into town, and as we sat back and reminisced over my grandfather's life, we realized that the way he lived and even the way he died was something we all aspired to. His life was rich in lessons learned and taught, and he died very peacefully, in the middle of the night, in his sleep. He had come to earth, loved the life he lived, and left a legacy.

Two nights before his funeral, some of our family was gathered at my grandparents' house and we were talking about how wonderful my grandfather was. His last living brother, the same one who had visited my parents' house just four weeks prior, was there, along with his wife and children. As we all shared, I told the family how I'd recently blogged about the lessons of life that my grandfather had taught me, most likely unbeknownst to them. They asked me to read the blog post to them, and after I did, they told me they wanted me to read the post during his funeral.

The next morning at the celebration-of-life service, all of us grandkids had a special role to play. Some of us spoke, and some of my male cousins were pallbearers. Each of us, when we went up to his casket, gave Granddaddy a soft peck somewhere on his face. He wasn't getting out of this world without getting some final tangible love from his grandkids and great-grandkids.

I then read what I had written about my grandfather:

What My Granddaddy Taught Me

Two mornings ago, I learned that one of my original heroes, my granddaddy, passed away in his sleep. He hadn't been sick, and in fact, two days before, he'd gone to the doctor and had received a great report. He passed away unexpectedly with no outward warning signs that he was getting ready to leave this earthly life. However, I am at peace knowing that he is with the Lord and that he left behind a legacy in our family that will never be erased.

In thinking of all the wonderful lessons I learned from him, I came up with the following seven that are prominent in my life. Hopefully you'll be able to apply these lessons to your life too.

1. It's okay to be different. Granddaddy was different. Not in a spooky kind of way but in the kind of way that you knew that he danced to the beat of his own drum. Granddaddy's greeting was "Howdy!" with a slight tilt of the head and a wave. I don't know of anyone else in this world who says "Howdy" on a daily basis except for my Granddaddy, and that's okay because that's what made him him. Granddaddy enjoyed wearing clothes with patches and he wore his pants up to or above his bellybutton! Granddaddy also thought it was necessary to only drive the regular streets (never the expressway) to get to where he was going. If you were on a car ride with Granddaddy, you knew you were going to be there for the long haul because your trip was going to take a while!

2. Love your spouse as if your life depended on it. My granddaddy took care of my grandma until the day he died. He cooked for her, cleaned for her, protected her, and provided companionship for her. Several years ago, my grandparents' house caught fire. My granddaddy knocked down a door to my grandparents' garage, grabbed a ladder, propped it up to the side of the house, climbed up to the second-floor bedroom window, and saved my grandmother. Talk about love.

3. Be an entrepreneur. For over forty years, my granddaddy, along with my grandma, owned and operated an upholstery shop. They knew the ins and outs of their industry, managed their business, and took care of their family. They landed contracts with some of the most well-known corporations in our city. They created wealth for themselves and didn't depend on anyone else to provide for them.

4. If it doesn't exist and you want it or need it, then build it. My granddaddy could build anything. Name it, and he could build it. From chairs to desks to bookshelves to television stands to whatever else you can think of, he could do it.

5. It's better to teach someone how to do something instead of doing it for them. I can remember moving into a new apartment when I was in my mid-twenties. The first-floor duplex's bedroom floors were hardwood, which were pretty but extremely cold in the wintertime since the bedrooms were directly above the garage. I asked my favorite carpenter/upholsterer/builder to help me lay carpet in the rooms so my feet wouldn't get cold. Instead of doing it for me, he took me to the big-box warehouse, taught me what kind of carpet I needed for the floor, brought me back to my apartment, and showed me exactly how to lay the carpet—and he left before I was even finished laying it all! "If you give a man a fish, you'll feed him for a day. If you teach a man how to fish, you'll feed him for a lifetime."

6. Time is precious currency. Spend it in a way that you'll have no regrets later. My granddaddy loved spending his time working on vehicles of all kinds. He got a kick out of building quirky-looking bird feeders and making use out of discarded goods. He enjoyed taking his grandkids fishing and bike riding, and most of all he enjoyed taking cross-country drives with his main gal, my grandma.

7. Tomorrow isn't promised—you better enjoy today. Three weeks before my granddaddy died, he spent time with his last surviving brother and his family. They laughed and talked and enjoyed each other's company. Ten days before he died, he was making my family smile because he was in his usual state, sitting on a stump outside of his house, underneath a tree sipping on a cold soda and just enjoying the warm summer day. The day before he died, he and my mom had a great phone conversation and made plans to go to a farmers' market later on in the week. All of us have plans to do things at some point in our lives, but don't wait until "some point" to start fulfilling your dreams, your purpose, and what God has promised in your heart.

My granddaddy was the true embodiment of "Live, Love, and Laugh." Life doesn't have to be complicated—we make it that way. Don't sweat the small stuff—after all, it's ALL small stuff. Love others, apologize when needed, forgive fast, and keep it moving. Thanks, Granddaddy, for teaching me the kind of stuff that money can't buy.

My granddaddy may be gone, but I will forever hold him and his love in my heart.

CHAPTER SIX

A month after my grandfather's funeral, we were readjusting to life. Chris was still working at the bank, but he told me his coworkers started to notice that, as a teller, he was a lot slower in counting money than other employees. He said he was going as fast as he could and that he was aiming for accuracy and not speed, but that they wanted him to move more quickly. In addition to that, his sales numbers were down. Way down. Even as a teller, he was expected to sell the bank's products and services to bank customers. He didn't feel that selling was his strong suit. "Babe," he would say, "I don't want to sell people debt. No one wants to take out another mortgage on their home or sign up for another credit card." I would encourage him by reminding him to continue doing the best he could and telling him I was sure it would all work out.

In the meantime, I had seriously started thinking about what it would mean to have an addition to our family. We had talked about it and we'd always land at the same place: I wanted two kids; Chris wanted one or none. I couldn't see myself not having any kids at all. I could possibly negotiate with Chris on the one-child idea, but no children at all wasn't an option for me. Up to this point, whenever someone asked us about having kids, we would always joke about it. But now, I was starting to think about how nice it would be to have a mini-me or a mini-Chris running around.

When people saw Chris and me, they saw big kids. We worked with the youth at our church and I was the girl who always knew she'd be a wife and a mom. I had served as a Vacation Bible School teacher for the church I grew up in, and I loved seeing the smiling faces of my students. Right after college, I was a Girl Scout troop leader for a group of scouts ages five to sixteen. In elementary school, I had tried to talk the girls on the playground into starting a real-life Baby-Sitters Club with me (like the one in some of my favorite books). Babysitting was my first job, and as a senior in college, I joined a baby-sitting registry and sat for kids to make extra money.

I loved kids, especially babies. I loved everything about them—their chubby cheeks, their sweet faces, the way their eyes lit up when they grasped a new concept or saw someone they knew. I loved when infants learned how to crawl and then, when they became toddlers, how they took joy in learning to walk. I enjoyed looking at cute little outfits in the stores and imagining what our children would look like. Chris and I would make great parents, and any kid who came into our world was going to have it made.

Five months before we got married, I asked my doctor to put me on birth control. Keep in mind that I was the chick who had decided to stay a virgin until marriage. I had heard from friends that when they first started birth control, they had to change it up a few times before they found one right for their bodies. So with their advice, I decided to start birth control five months *before* Chris and I got married. I knew I eventually wanted kids, but the thought of losing my virginity and getting pregnant the night I got married was way too much for me to handle. I figured if my birth control got set into my body just right, by the time Chris and I got married, I'd be good to go in terms of getting it on with my new husband and staying kid-free for a while.

But when I started seriously thinking about us getting pregnant, I didn't know what to do. I mean, was there a method to coming off birth control? And how long would it take to get pregnant? And did I need to change anything in my lifestyle before I got pregnant? All of these questions were swirling in my head, and there was only one person who could answer any of the questions adequately for me: my doctor. I trusted her and I loved her. She had always given me good advice, and when I would ask her a million and one questions (like I planned to this time), she would just look at me, shake her head, and tell me the truth according to what the medical facts were—as opposed to what my racing mind was telling me.

Over the last seven years, my doctor and I had developed a special relationship. She always greeted me with a smile and a chuckle. I told her I knew I was her favorite patient so many times that even she started calling me her favorite patient. She was wonderful and I was grateful to have found her on a whim years before, all because I had a sinus infection. A lot of doctors didn't have a very good bedside manner, but she did. I knew she actually cared about me, and that she wouldn't tell me something that wasn't best for me. So I prepped all of my "getting off birth control" questions for her and made an appointment for August 2014.

During my appointment, the doctor answered *all* of my questions about baby-making preparations. She told me my husband and I weren't getting any younger and that if we were ready to start a family, to go for it. She told me that if I wanted to stop taking birth control that it was as easy as not taking another pill. I laughed at myself when she said that. Here I was thinking there was a process to stopping birth control, but all I had to do was stop taking it!

But as she moved on from my questions into the comprehensive annual exam, she told me she was concerned about something she saw in my chart. She noticed that after the negative results from the biopsy on my left breast in November 2013, I hadn't gone back for a follow-up mammogram, ultrasound, and MRI like I was supposed to. She told me that before I started trying to have a baby, I needed to go for my follow-up exams.

I sighed and told her, "okay," but only because it was her. If it was important enough for her to tell me to do it, I figured I should do it. My whole reason for not going in the first place was because I thought I was healthy enough to not go. I'd already had a biopsy the year prior, and the doctors said I didn't have cancer, so did I *really* need to do the six-month follow-up exam? The doctors told me that what they found were fibroadenomas, just small, benign tumors. The biopsy proved that my health wasn't at risk, so did I *really* need to go? Plus, I was tired of having that big, heavy machine push on my boobs.

But when the doctor told me to go—and when she said I needed to do it before we started trying to have kids—I decided to listen. Almost overnight I went from joking about having kids to doing everything I could to make sure we would have a healthy baby.

A few days later, I scheduled my follow-up appointments to take place on a Friday. Having my boobs squished, pressed down, assaulted by gel and machinery, and getting pictures taken of them sounded taxing. If all of that was going to happen, I really wanted to get it done in one day.

I had the mammogram first. The room was cold, my gown wouldn't stay on, and the tech was sweet as could be, but every time she told me to "hold my breath" in her deep Southern accent as the mammogram machine snapped a picture, I couldn't help but think of Dolly Parton. How appropriate, right? Next was the sonogram. *Really, are we really doing this?* I thought. The sonogram tech squirted warm gel out of a tube on each of my breasts and examined them one at a time. I could see a ton of squiggly lines on the black screen. Every few seconds she would stop moving and use a tool on her computer keyboard to measure whatever she saw. I remember my doctor telling me I had very dense breast tissue, which could make it hard to see malignant issues, so I didn't mind the tech taking the extra time.

After that appointment, I went to the MRI facility. I'd never gotten an MRI before, and I wasn't looking forward to the one I needed to have. Lying on the MRI machine facedown and listening to the loud knocking noises the machine made when it took pictures made my chest and ears hurt. This was becoming too much. Did I really need to go through all of this? After all, I believed I was healthy.

The following Monday, I returned to work with the expectation of getting the results back sometime that week. In my perfect world, the results would come back and prove that everything was completely normal, that my tests from the previous Friday were just precautionary, and that I could really start talking to my husband about when he thought it would be good to make a baby.

That Wednesday, I got the news I didn't want to hear. "Mrs. Jones," the voice on the phone said, "we need you to come back for a follow-up appointment."

"For what?" I asked, not really wanting to know the answer.

"Well, we found something that concerns us, and we just want to check it out one more time," the woman explained.

"Oh Lord, here we go again," I said while rolling my eyes. "That's fine. What's your first available appointment?" I asked. She told me to call the scheduling center and that she thought I'd be able to get back in fairly soon. I made my appointment for that Friday, and I dreaded having to get another ultrasound.

Speaking of which, why did these tests *have* to take place in the cancer center, anyway? I mean, I didn't have cancer. All I was doing was getting mammograms and ultrasounds, and the doctors wanted to examine my dense breast tissue to make sure I didn't have cancer. Couldn't those appointments happen in other parts of the hospital? I could understand why patients who had been diagnosed with cancer had to go to that particular building, but for people who hadn't been diagnosed with cancer, couldn't we have gone somewhere else?

At my appointment the following week, the sonogram tech had me lie on another hospital bed; she kept on all the lights and rubbed the sonogram tool over my right breast.

"What do you see?" I asked.

"Well, I see a few things, and for a better idea of what's really going on, I think you're going to need to come back for a biopsy," she said.

"Are you serious? Another one? I just had a biopsy done on my left breast last year. Do I really have to come back for another one for the right side?" I asked, taking a deep breath.

"Yes, ma'am. We prefer that you come back just to make sure that there's nothing wrong," she told me. Letting out a deep sigh and yet again being at the mercy of a medical professional, I obliged. "I'll make my appointment before I leave the office today." I scheduled the biopsy for the following Monday and left the center.

Leaving the office, I couldn't help but question, *How did I find myself here all over again?* I was just here ten months ago, and here I was again, about to go through the painful sting of getting a needle biopsy done to ensure I didn't have cancer. Chris and I prepared ourselves again for me to lie on the table with the medical professionals surrounding me while Chris was in the waiting room.

The only good thing about having a second needle biopsy was that I knew how to prepare for my appointment. This time around,

I made sure to have music on my phone that I could listen to as the doctor poked me. And since I knew about the anesthetic stinging, I brought a couple of stress-reliever balls with me to squeeze tightly so I wouldn't almost crush the nurse's hand I held during the procedure.

During the biopsy, as I lay on the table, looking up at the ceiling with the doctors and nurses around me, I had contemporary Christian and gospel songs playing loudly into my ears. It was me and Jesus on that table, and as long as I could hear positivity coming through my headphones, I was okay.

I joked around with the nurses and doctors, and they got the fluid from the fibroadenomas they needed. I felt especially comfortable because the same two nurses who were with me only a year prior were with me this time around too. One of them remembered me squeezing her hand very tightly. I apologized to her, and she said that was what she was there for.

As the doctors and nurses finished, I figured I'd ask a pressing question that was on my mind. The two female nurses and male doctor who performed the biopsy procedure had left the room, and only one other doctor and I were left behind. She was gathering the final pieces of information she needed to complete the biopsy and telling me what I needed to know before I left the procedure room.

"So," I said to the doctor, "I know you all said for me to get a follow-up MRI in six months. But what happens if I get pregnant?"

"Don't," she said. I knew pregnant women couldn't get MRIs because the contrast that is used can cause a spontaneous abortion.

"Yeah, but what if I do?" I pressed the question.

"I would recommend that you wait beyond the six months to get pregnant," she said.

"But what if I get pregnant before then?" I asked again.

"Well, we would prefer that you wait and go in for the follow-up

MRI so that we can make sure that you are completely free of any issues before you get pregnant," she said.

I told her "okay" and didn't ask my question again.

The following week, I returned to work on Wednesday and was getting back into my usual routine. In the middle of the week, I got a call from the doctor who did the actual biopsy. He had my test results back, and I was ready to hear them.

"Mrs. Jones," he said, "we tested five spots that were of concern to us."

"Really?" I asked with my mouth dropping.

"Yes, two of them were no problem, just like we thought. Two of them are fibroadenomas, and we aren't concerned about those either. But there's one that's called an intraductal papilloma and it's growing in one of your milk ducts in your right breast," he said.

"It's a *what*?" I asked. All I heard was "intra-something" and that it was growing in my milk duct. Beyond that, I didn't know what he was talking about.

"Well, it's called an intraductal papilloma," he said. "It's not cancerous—however, in patients like yourself, who have a history of breast cancer in their family, it can put you at a 10 percent higher chance of developing breast cancer over the course of your lifetime."

Everything in me went silent.

"So, what are my options?" I asked him very directly.

"Well, you can either have it surgically removed, or you can leave it there, we can watch it, and see what happens."

Almost without thinking, I quickly responded, "This isn't a viewing party. I don't want to 'sit and watch it'; I want it removed."

"Okay," he said.

"When is your earliest appointment?" I asked with a sense of urgency.

He told me to call the schedulers in the department to get the surgery scheduled. I heeded his instructions as soon as I got off the phone.

I called Chris to tell him what was going on, and as usual, he was encouraging and told me not to worry and that God would prevail in the situation. The next person I wanted to talk to was my mom. She had gone through the various appointments I had gone through, and I trusted her judgment on this situation. After all, she was a cancer survivor. In her case, at her very first mammogram, just like the morning show reporter, the doctors found that she had pre-stage I cancer cells in her right breast. Since the doctors had found this "intra-thingy" in my right breast too, I knew I wanted it removed. I remember being twelve years old when she and my dad told my brother and me that she was diagnosed with breast cancer. It scared me. She had gotten a mastectomy to make sure the cancer didn't return in her breast, and at this point, if this "intra-thingy" could lead to anything that sounded like cancer, I was willing to cut it and my entire breast off if I needed to.

"Mom," I said when I called her.

"Hi, Daughter," she responded cheerfully.

"Can I talk to you for a second?" I asked.

"Sure, what's going on?"

I went on to tell her about the biopsy results and what the doctor said. I told her I was planning to have the surgery to remove the intraductal papilloma, and my mom was in full agreement with me.

"You're right," she told me. "If it can put you at risk, you definitely don't want to leave it in there."

I told her I'd be over to visit her and my dad later that week. I felt good about my decision. This intraductal thing would be out of my breast and out of my life in a matter of two weeks. Chris was keeping me positive about the situation, and I felt in control of my health.

+ + +

The next day, my brother texted me. "*Hey, did you know that Dad is planning on taking Fefe to put her to sleep tonight?*" Fefe was my parents' eleven-year-old dog that we had all fallen in love with over a decade ago when my brother and dad decided to get her while my mom was out of town one weekend and I was in college. "*What?*" I texted back.

For the last several weeks, Fefe hadn't been herself. She was a purebred Shih Tzu that was typically overly hyper. If dogs had emotions and could be happy, Fefe was super-happy. But at the same time, she could be calm and laid-back. In a lot of ways, she had taken on the personality of our family. But over the last several weeks, she seemed lethargic and moped around a lot. Originally we thought that maybe her leg was bothering her. A few years prior, she had been diagnosed with a hernia, so we thought maybe that was the issue. But this was different. Our normally happy and hyper dog was sad and seemed to be in pain. At the constant urging of my mom, my dad had decided to take her to the vet for a checkup, and it was discovered that she had cancer. Her health quickly declined, and by the day my brother texted me, my dad had made the decision that no pet lover or owner wants to make—he'd decided to put Fefe to sleep.

I knew that decision was one of the hardest my dad ever had to make. Being the close-knit family we were, my brother and I wanted to make sure we spent some time loving on Fefe before her vet appointment. In a lot of ways, Fefe was like a four-legged sibling to us. She got excited when she saw us and always jumped up and down when we got ready to play with her or take her outside. At the sight of her leash, she'd run around in circles and start barking with a loud squeal because she knew she was going outside. Fefe was a dog lover's dream, and it was sad we were going to have to put our little buddy down.

My brother and I met my parents at their house that night. We decided that my dad, my brother, and I would go to the vet together. When we arrived, Fefe didn't want to get out of the car. It was as if she knew that day would be her final one.

A veterinarian came and got us from the waiting room, and my dad carried Fefe back to one of the examination rooms. The three of us sat in the room and reminisced about how much fun we'd had with Fefe through the years. Though my mom initially didn't like our four-legged friend very much, she had grown to love her. And through the years, Fefe had made all of us laugh. She had brought joy to our family.

When the veterinarian asked us what brought us in that night, my dad explained through a choked-up voice and with tears in his eyes that Fefe had been diagnosed with cancer and that none of the medications she had been prescribed would improve her health. In fact, the veterinarians were pretty much at their last options when it came to treatment plans. My dad's choices were to keep her on medication to alleviate some of her pain, or he could put her to sleep. She hadn't been our normal Girlie, or Doggie, or FeeeeFeeee; she was a sad dog who had done her service to her human family, and it was time for her to rest. So the veterinarian started the process of euthanization while my dad, brother, and I took turns holding Fefe, telling her how much we loved her and how grateful we were to have her. We laughed about how my mom didn't initially want her and how she later fell in love with her, and we told her she was the best dog we could've ever wished for. We took pictures with her, we all stood around and cried, and after she took her last breath, my dad asked me if I'd pray for our family and our beloved Fefe. The veterinarian joined in with us and told us how lucky Fefe was to have had us and that she could tell how much she was loved. My dad, brother, and I left the animal hospital sad, but we knew our precious Fefe was now out of pain.

In some of the pictures we took with Fefe that night, a piece of gauze from my recent biopsy could be seen. I'd had it only four days prior, and I still needed to cover it up every day. I'd tried to hide most of it in the pictures, but a small piece of it stuck out from underneath my dress, reminding me and apparently my dad that I needed to go home and chill out. It had been a rough week on me mentally and physically, and in exactly three weeks, I'd be undergoing the first surgery of my life.

"Baby girl," my dad said, "go home and get some rest."

"Yes, sir," I said, giving him a hug.

+ + +

Over the next two weeks, I prepped myself for surgery. I made sure I was as healthy as possible and mentally ready to have the intraductal papilloma removed. I'd taken off from work on the day of the surgery and the next day and planned to go back to work on the following Monday. Chris was still working at the bank and I assured him I would be fine. He dropped me off at the hospital that morning, and my mom and grandma met me there shortly after. I'd never had surgery so I had no idea what to expect, but it seemed like an adventure to me—almost like I was gaining a badge of honor. The clinical resident who would be assisting the main surgeon came in to visit with me and explained everything that would be happening. I felt at ease with her because she was around my age and was so nice. After she left us and told me that the anesthesiologist would soon be in to see me, my mom suggested that she, my grandma, and I pray. She prayed for my health, for the hands of the surgeons, and that all would be well with us. She prayed with passion and with fervor. She prayed, and I believed.

When I woke up from surgery, I was groggy and a little out of it. My mom was right there smiling at me from the end of the bed, and my grandma was next to me. Two of my favorite girls in the world were beside me, and that felt good. I got a little sick from the anesthesia after I woke up, but for the most part, I'd made it through surgery just fine. The doctor let me know that they'd removed the intraductal papilloma and I was good to go.

That evening, my mom and her mom took me home, and shortly after we arrived, my dad's mom and sister showed up to check on me. At that point, I had four of my favorite girls all together with me in my house. My family was my world, and it meant so much to have them there with me. We sat there and laughed and talked about all of the crazy stories that were on the evening news that night. We enjoyed each other's company, and I felt blessed to have four of the most important women in my life with me on the day of my surgery.

Chris got home a few hours later and relieved the women in my family of their nursing duties. He made sure I was okay and that I was taking it easy. He told me he felt bad for not coming to the hospital with me, but I assured him I was fine. I had encouraged him to go to work that day, and I had told him that my mom and grandmas and aunt would be coming to take care of me.

"Yeah, but I should've been there," he said reflectively.

"But I am okay. And you are here now, and that's what matters," I told him.

Honestly, I just wanted to make sure that he stayed in good standing with his job. I knew I had family who would come and take care of me, and I felt like we'd gone through so much when he didn't have a job for eighteen and a half months that I didn't want us to ever be in that space again. Over the last few weeks, he had started telling me how yet again he hadn't been able to meet his sales goals at the bank and was concerned he might get fired. In addition to that, some of the coworkers he had started with had either been transferred to other banks or had been fired. He was becoming nervous about his performance at work, and I was becoming nervous about him possibly losing his job again.

As I healed and returned to work, I thought about all of the experiences Chris and I had been through over the last few months. My grandfather had passed away unexpectedly, I'd gone through all of the medical appointments, which ultimately led to surgery, and Fefe had died.

In addition to all of this, Chris's nurse practitioner (who focused on his MS diagnosis and well-being) decided to change his medication from an every-other-day injectable shot to a monthly infusion. The infusion part sounded a little intimidating, but we knew that if it was for his health to be in the best condition, we would be okay. The part that bothered us was when the doctor told us that the only side effect of the medication was that sometimes people developed a brain infection. The nurse practitioner assured us that Chris would be tested regularly for the virus that could lead to the infection, and as long as those tests were negative, we would be fine. The second half of 2014 was turning out to be one big roller coaster. But God was still good. We had our family, our jobs, our friends, and each other.

The more I started thinking about it, the more I tried to figure out how in the world—or why in the world, for that matter—those "things," those fibroadenomas, the intraductal papilloma, were showing up in my breasts. I was a typically healthy thirty-one-year-old woman. I didn't drink, I didn't smoke, I didn't engage in dangerous activities, and yet these "things" were popping up. I started doing some research, and according to some sources, I read that increased estrogen could possibly play a role in a woman's breast health.

The only increased estrogen I had was coming through the birth control pills that I was taking every day. Initially, when I started birth control in January 2011, the doctor and I agreed that I would be on it for only two years and then I'd get off. Because of my mother's breast cancer history, the doctor prescribed only low-dose pills. In 2011, two years of birth control sounded like a good amount of time. I thought Chris and I would be ready to have a baby in 2013. But when 2013 came, Chris and I were still trying to get settled into married life. Neither of us felt ready to become parents at the time, and Chris was between jobs. And beyond that, Chris had been diagnosed with MS and doctors found the first set of fibroadenomas in my breast. We just weren't ready for me to stop taking birth control.

But here we were in 2014, and I was ready to come off the pills. Now that I was reading about how estrogen could possibly play a negative role in breast health, I was especially eager to make the change. At the same time, the research I read online was inconclusive, and for every paper I found that said estrogen could play a harmful role in breast health, I found another paper that said estrogen didn't play a harmful role in it. Whatever the case, I had decided that after my next period ended, I wasn't going to take any more birth control pills. I had talked to Chris about it, and though he wasn't completely sold on the idea of possibly getting pregnant, he was okay with my decision because I felt strongly about it and we were talking about my health.

CHAPTER SEVEN

Two weeks after surgery, I started to realize I was overdoing it. While walking around the medical center one day at work, I started to feel weak and light-headed, like I was going to faint. I hadn't taken off a lot of time after the biopsy or the surgery, and it was all starting to catch up with me. It didn't help that my monthly cycle had started that Monday. So in addition to my body being tired from the recent surgery, it was also tired from my period. That upcoming weekend, I was to be in a good friend's wedding, and I decided that all of the wedding activities plus the way I had been feeling were probably good reasons for me to request time off from work. I put in my official request and planned to be off that Friday and the following Monday. That Friday, I'd get my hair and nails done in preparation for the big event that was happening on Saturday, and on Monday, I'd have a chance to relax.

That weekend was awesome. My friend and her new husband were a fun-loving couple whom Chris and I had hung out with several times before. We'd double-date and go to the movies, bowl, or have dinner together. They were a great couple and their wedding party was full of great people. Recently, it seemed as if all of us had been through some type of crazy life situation, but we all managed to bounce back. I was the youngest of the seven bridesmaids, and as we spent time together that weekend, we talked about the various stages of life we were in. Some of us were married; a few of the girls were dating; some of the women had kids. To me, that diversity was what made us such a great group. We celebrated our friends in style that night and wished them well as they started on their new journey as husband and wife. Little did I know, but that weekend was the start of a new journey for Chris and me too—one that would completely change the course of our lives.

+ + +

That Sunday, Chris and I relaxed, just as planned, and on Monday I planned on doing the same thing. But God had other plans.

Any time I took off a day from work, I always liked to sleep in. Besides, on this particular "off" day, that's all I planned to do anyway. Relax. Sleep. Watch TV. Eat. Repeat. And not necessarily in that order. My body was tired, I was tired, and I was ready to just be lazy.

On November 10, at 11:04 a.m., my phone rang on my nightstand, waking me. I grabbed my phone to see who was calling and if I really needed to answer. It was Chris. He was the only person who could've called me that day and gotten me to answer the phone.

"Babe, I was just in a car accident, and I need for you to come get me," Chris said.

"You were *what*?" I exclaimed.

Chris was always playing practical jokes, and I thought surely this had to have been a joke.

"I was just in a car accident, and I need you to come get me," he repeated.

By this time, I had gotten out of bed, phone in hand, and I ran over to the bedroom window to see if both our vehicles were in the driveway. Sure enough, Chris's SUV was not.

"Okay. Are you okay?" I asked, feeling scared and nervous.

"I'm okay; I just need you to come and get me," he said.

"Okay—tell me where you are and I'll be on my way."

As I drove to get Chris, I didn't know what to think. He said he was okay, but Chris always said he was okay. Nothing ever seemed to shake him. When he told me the stretch of the highway that he was on when the accident occurred, I knew it was a very busy part of the interstate near a merge ramp. I didn't know if someone had merged into his car or if someone was going too fast and had slammed on their brakes, hitting him, or if he had run off the road. Had he blacked out on the highway? Or maybe he was going too fast and had hit someone. My mind was racing.

When I got to the gas station where Chris told me to go, he and a police officer were there. As I approached them, the police officer turned to Chris and told him, "You're lucky to be alive." As he said those words, I could feel my heart starting to beat faster and my eyes widening. The police officer went on, "So, the police report will be ready at some point this week. It could've been much worse," he said. And then he mentioned something about children being involved in the accident.

Oh, my God, I thought. *What happened?*

As we got into my car and buckled our seat belts, I turned to Chris. "I'm so glad you're okay," I told him. And then I asked my million-dollar question, "What happened?"

"Well, there was an animal that ran into the road and I swerved to avoid hitting it," he said. "When I did that, I bounced off a guard rail and ended up hitting another car, and that caused my car to roll over on the highway." Every detail of the accident sounded as scary to me as it probably was for Chris. "When I was rolling in the air, I thought angels were going to come and get me," he said. And then with a big grin, he said, "I was looking for them, but they never came."

Pulling into our driveway, I turned to him and said, "You *what*?"

"Well, yeah, I was expecting for angels to come for me 'cause I thought I was gonna die, but they never showed up."

Though relieved, I thought, *I should punch him for being so casual about what had just happened!*

"So, do you have pictures of how bad this accident was?" I asked.

"Yeah, there are some on my phone."

When he handed me his phone, I looked in utter disbelief at what had occurred. Chris's charcoal-gray Envoy had landed on its hood, and glass surrounded the vehicle. The front half of the car was smashed down, touching the ground, while the back half teetered in the air. It was amazing he had survived that type of impact. He explained that the other car had two women and three children in it and some of them were transported to a hospital via ambulance for observation. He thought they would be okay.

Looking at the picture in disbelief, I uttered, "How did you get out of *this*?" referring to the completely totaled car.

"Well, a good samaritan pulled over and helped me climb out of the back passenger side of the car," he told me. Characteristic of Chris, he went on to say with a laugh, "I bet you thought I was gonna die today, huh?"

Looking at him with a blank face, I asked, "What are you talking about?"

"I bet when you learned I was in a car accident, you thought I was gonna die today, but I'm still here, which means you won't get my insurance money," he said with a laugh.

"Are you freaking kidding me?" I yelled. "Of course, I didn't think you were going to die, and no, I'm not after your insurance money!"

Chuckling, he replied, "Well, since I didn't die, you definitely aren't going to get it today!" He then walked away from me and went upstairs, saying he had to send some additional information to the police who had covered the accident. I stood in the living room, numb over the fact that my husband had almost died on that day and that he was joking with me about insurance money. I had a hard time believing he could make light of what happened.

Chris is a situational comedian who can make a joke out of any circumstance. He is different from anyone else I have ever met. Everything is black and white with him, and there are no shades of gray. His yes is yes and his no is no, and there is no in between. And though sometimes his straightforwardness and his joking can be off-putting for some, most of the time it helps balance our household. When I try to tiptoe around issues, he confronts them head on, and when I am too serious, he always finds a way to make us both laugh. Occasionally, depending on the circumstance, that same straightforwardness or joking that balances us can be almost too much for me to handle—but I love him nonetheless.

About an hour after we got home from his accident, he told me he needed to go to the store to get food to make for dinner. I sat in our spare bedroom speechless about him having literally almost died.

I started to feel the tears roll down my face. As if we hadn't already been through enough over the last few months, a serious car accident was not something we needed. Plus, my husband was saying he was fine, but what about this other family? I mean, were they really going to be all right? Were they injured, too? Did Chris just say they were okay because he thought they were? My mind was racing. After all of this happening, I decided I was going to need an extra day off work to bounce back from this first day off work.

As my mind wandered, I couldn't help but think about the recent pregnancy conversation I'd had with my doctor. Here it was November, and just three months prior I had been discussing with her the idea of getting off birth control to have a baby. But how on earth would I be able to focus on having a baby with me having just had surgery to remove a spot from my breast? And now, with this car accident, we would be down to one car until we could buy another one. The more I started to think about it, the more I started to realize that maybe it wasn't the best time for us to conceive. I couldn't bring a child into all of this stressful mess with a clear conscience. I wouldn't dare do that to a baby. I wouldn't dare do that to me or Chris. No way. I called the doctor that afternoon and told her to please call in another three-month supply of birth control to the pharmacy.

I took two pills that night and took another one the next day. But as I sat in a parking lot on that Wednesday, I had an epiphany. *There is never a perfect time to have a baby, Danielle,* I thought to myself. *There will never be enough money; things will never be completely perfect. And if you wait, you will always have an excuse to not get pregnant.* And I still wasn't sure if the birth control was causing the fibroadenomas in my breasts. I didn't know what effects the extra estrogen was having on my body. At that point, I was almost two years beyond the stopping point my doctor and I had initially agreed upon. I took a deep sigh and decided at that moment that I had taken the last birth control pill I was going to take.

I called my husband and asked him if he had time to talk.

"Sure, babe. What's up?" he asked me.

I explained to him my thought process and how I was definitely ready to come off birth control. I had already talked with my doctor about non-hormonal birth control options. Another option was to get an insert placed into my skin that would allow the birth control medication to slowly release every month. It sounded minimally invasive, but both Chris and I had hesitations. I was sure I would want to have babies soon, and I wasn't looking for a long-term birth control option. Plus, Chris didn't like the idea of me going through any other type of physical procedure.

"Babe, your body has been through enough," he said. "I don't want you to go through any other pain."

While we had decided for me to stop taking birth control pills, we also decided that we didn't want to use any other means of protection. We weren't going to intentionally try to get pregnant, but we weren't doing anything to prevent it either. We wanted me to be healthy and we wanted our lives to just "be." And if that included a child, we would be fine with that.

As the month went on and things started to settle down for us, Chris decided to resign from the bank where he was working. He didn't want to get let go like he did from his last job, and he already knew that his sales numbers were down. He had been searching for another opportunity for a few weeks and had found what he thought was a good fit at a warehouse. We had gotten another car to replace the SUV that had been totaled in the accident. And one of my parents' church members actually knew the two women and children who were in the other car that was involved in Chris's car accident. Thankfully, the family was physically fine. They hadn't been injured in the car accident, and they were doing well.

As Thanksgiving came and went that year, we had a lot to be grateful for. My surgery had gone well and Chris was alive, despite being in a horrific car accident. He was going to start a new job that he felt more confident about and we seemed to be turning a corner. As we entered into December, things were going well.

CHAPTER EIGHT

As a teenage girl and then into adulthood, my period came like clockwork. Honestly, you could tell time by the thing. Once it had figured out its cycle, it stuck to it. I knew a lot of girls took birth control to regulate their periods, but not me. I didn't need to. Ol' "Flo" was as faithful as they came. But over the last month, when I'd taken the three birth control pills after Chris's car accident and then stopped taking them, I bled lightly for a couple of days and then just stopped. I called my doctor to ask her about it and she told me it was because my body was reacting to me stopping, then starting, then stopping the birth control again. She also told me that next time, I should just finish the whole pack so my body wouldn't be thrown off by the hormones in the pills.

But three weeks later, "Flo" didn't show up on the day she was supposed to. I also found I wasn't hungry in the morning like I usually was, but instead I was hungry later in the day. I started thinking that there was a chance I could be pregnant. So, I went to buy a pregnancy test.

As I stood in the drug store, there were so many options and so many brand names. How was I supposed to know which one to get? I didn't want to waste my money and get a less expensive one and it be wrong, but I also didn't want to get the most expensive one and waste my money if there wasn't truly a bun growing in my oven. And some of the tests had pluses and minuses, while others had one line or two lines to let a couple know if they were indeed pregnant. This was serious business, and I knew that the lines and the pluses and minuses may have tripped me up. I was smart, but I was also a little goofy, and in this case, anything with a plus or a minus or any type of line through it or on it probably wasn't my best bet. As I studied all of the test options, I came across a digital one that was pretty reasonably priced, and it clearly read "Pregnant" or "Not Pregnant." Like most pregnancy tests, there were two kits in the box in case I wanted to take the test twice. *Perfect*, I thought. If my period didn't show up by the next morning, I was prepared to take a pregnancy test and find out if Chris and I were about to become parents.

The next morning, I got ready for church; Chris was planning to stream church and then watch a football game. But before our morning could truly start, I knew I needed to take one of the pregnancy tests. I took the test and set it on the counter, thinking I would need to wait three to five minutes before I got the results. But almost instantly, the little screen flashed "Pregnant," and at that moment I knew Chris and I were in for the wildest ride of our lives. I stared at myself in the mirror with my hand cupped over my mouth. I couldn't believe it; Chris and I were going to have a baby. I quietly got dressed, smiling ear to ear and half in disbelief. As I prepared to leave home that morning, Chris was still asleep. I kissed him on his forehead and tiptoed out the door.

I was actually pregnant. What in the world? I mean, I wanted to get pregnant. I know the breast doctor suggested that I not, because I'd need to get an MRI in a few months, but we were thirty-one and thirty-two. It just felt like it was the right time for us to have a baby. And as a close family member had put it, if we continued to wait, we'd only be older and wishing we'd already gotten pregnant. Besides, getting pregnant now would just mean that I'd have to wait some extra months before my next MRI, which I was completely fine with doing. But, seriously, we were pregnant. Like really pregnant. Chris and I were going to be somebody's parents. Wow.

Driving to church that morning, I wasn't quite sure how to tell Chris. Every few minutes that I drove, the thought came to me: "Oh my gosh, we're going to have a baby! Oh, my gosh, we're going to have a baby!" My mind went into overdrive. I had been dreaming about being a mom since I was a little girl. I would have two to three kids—definitely no more than three, because if I had three, they'd already outnumber me and their father. And it didn't really matter if I had a girl or a boy. I could play with doll babies or I could go to football games; I didn't care as long as I had kids! And now, I was going to be a mom and Chris was going to be a dad. I couldn't wait. I started thinking about all of the fun stuff we'd do as a family and the places we'd go. Wow. We were going to be parents. But as I relished in that, I had to think of a great way to tell Chris. I pulled up at church and touched my stomach and smiled. "Your daddy isn't going to believe this!"

Church was awesome that morning. The pastor preached from the first chapter of Luke about how God could perform miracles and how when Mary learned she was pregnant with Jesus, she met up with Elizabeth. Elizabeth was pregnant also, and as the two cousins got together, Elizabeth's baby jumped inside of her. The pastor challenged us to believe that God was going to perform a miracle in our lives.

After church, I got my plan together for telling Chris the news. Chris was an avid Cincinnati Bengals fan, so I picked out some unisex Onesies with the Bengals mascot and was ready to put my plan into action.

When I got home, I hurried upstairs and laid out the clothes along with Chris's Bengals jersey on the bed. I made a sign and set it next to the display of jerseys that read, "Merry Christmas, Daddy! I can't wait to watch the games with you next year!" I also put the pregnancy test that still read "Pregnant" next to the sign. Chris was in for the surprise of his life, and I couldn't wait to see his face.

He was downstairs watching a Bengals game when I called him upstairs to see my display. I yelled for him to come up, and as he peeped his head into our bedroom, I directed his attention to the bed.

"Read the sign!" I said with a huge grin on my face. He read the sign slowly and then looked up at me with big eyes.

"What are you trying to say?" he asked me, as if he knew what I was trying to tell him but couldn't believe it.

"What does the sign say?" I asked him, chuckling.

He read the sign again, slowly, and then looked at the pregnancy test. He looked at me again.

"I'm pregnant! You're going to be a daddy!"

"Nuh-uh!" he exclaimed, while laughing.

"Yeah, you are! I'm going to be a mommy and you're going to be a daddy!" I told him excitedly.

"I don't believe you!" he said, with equal parts excitement and skepticism in his voice.

"Really! I'm pregnant!" I said in a high-pitched tone. "I have another pregnancy test if you want me to take it!" I said, knowing the test would come back positive.

"Yeah, I want you to take the test again!"

"Okay, fine. I will!" I told him. I ran to the bathroom to take the test and left him in the bedroom to try to get over his disbelief that I was actually pregnant.

To ensure he saw the proof, after taking the test and washing my hands, I emerged from the bathroom with the test in my hand and gave it to him. No sooner than I did, the digital display started flashing "Pregnant."

"I can't believe it," he said, staring at the test.

"Yep, you're going to be a daddy! If you want me to, I'll even go to the doctor and get a blood test. Those things are foolproof!"

"Yes, I want you to go get a blood test," Chris told me, still not totally believing I was pregnant.

Two days after taking my at-home pregnancy test, I went to my doctor. Before she even offered me a blood test, she told me to take another traditional pregnancy test. Before the test results could even register all the way, she and her assistant smiled at me and told me what I already knew: "You are definitely pregnant!" her assistant said.

"There's no doubt about it. Your hormone numbers are off the charts," said the doctor, smiling. She had known all of the twists and turns that our lives had taken during the recent months, and she knew Chris and I believed in God and His purpose. "This must all be a part of God's divine plan," she said, giving me a hug. "I believe it too!"

Just to make sure Chris knew that I wasn't playing with him, that I didn't buy faulty pregnancy tests, and that he was definitely going to be a daddy, I called him from the doctor's office and put him on speaker phone. "Hey, babe!" I said, laughing, "The doctor wants to talk with you!" I put my doctor on the phone.

"She's definitely pregnant!" she said.

Now with the final confirmation, Chris said, "I guess all of you can't be wrong. I guess she really is pregnant!"

After getting Chris to actually accept the fact that I was pregnant, I went into planning mode for how I was going to tell our families.

I'd been thinking about this day for a long time. I remember a college classmate telling me that when she and her fiancé found out they were pregnant, they gave their parents cards with their new titles on them. I always liked that idea and thought our families would too. But I wanted to do something a little bit extra. I gave them all cards with their new titles, and I wrote little notes to all of them from their future nephew, niece, or grandchild. I had also downloaded a pregnancy app so I could get 3-D glimpses of what the baby looked like every week, and I printed off pictures of what a six-week-old gestational baby would look like and put them in everyone's card.

Our baby would be the sixth grandchild on Chris's side of the family, and he or she would be the first grandchild on my side of the family. It was as if the stars had aligned and God had planned it so that this little person would be our families' Christmas miracle.

We received memorable reactions from our families. We decided to tell my family on my dad's birthday, which is Christmas Eve. We passed around our little gift bags and let everyone open them and figure out that we were pregnant. My brother and my cousin jumped up and down and gave me the biggest hugs and slapped Chris on his back; my parents turned red, and both of them exclaimed, "Whoooaaaa! We're going to be grandparents!" after reading their cards and re-reading them; Chris's brother and sister-in-law laughed at us and told us to get ready to have our lives changed forever; Chris's mom screamed out of joy from the top of her lungs; Chris's dad repeated, "Well that's all right, that's all right," and laughed to himself; and Chris's two young nieces were excited to learn that they would be big cousins. But my eighty-year-old grandmother on my mom's side of the family and my eighty-five-year-old grandma on my dad's side took the cake when it came to touching responses to learning about their unborn great-grandchild.

I gave my mom's mom a small gift bag with a word-find puzzle book, a card, and a bib that said, "Grandma's Dream Come True." It seemed like my mother's mother wanted me to have a baby more than Chris and I even wanted to have a baby. She had ten grandkids and more than twenty great-grandkids, yet for the last few years, most of the times when she saw me, she was asking me if Chris and I were "working on putting a bun in the oven," if we "had anything cooking," and if we "knew how to work [our] parts right," whatever that meant! She really wanted this great-grandchild, and finally her wishes were coming true. The card I gave her read, "Dear Great Grandma, I can't wait to meet you! Thank you so much for praying for me! Obviously, prayer really works! Even though Great Grandpa isn't physically here this Christmas, I hope me coming next year brings you joy! P.S. I can't wait to do crossword puzzles with you! Love, Little Baby Jones."

My mom, overly excited and giddy, read my grandma's card out loud to her and shouted to her mother, "Mommy, they're having a baby! You're going to be a great-grandma again!" My grandma sat frozen in the corner of the couch as tears streamed down her face. The sixth of her nine grandbabies was having a baby.

The next day, my dad's side of the family gathered at his mom's house, and I gave small bags to both his mom and his sister. My grandmother's card read "Dear Great Grandma, I can't wait to meet you! When I get here, we'll have to watch the baseball games and get ice cream together! Love ya, Li'l Baby Jones." My grandmother on my father's side of the family was a huge baseball fan. In fact, just four weeks prior to our pregnancy announcement, I had taken her to an event at which hometown baseball fans could meet former and current Cincinnati Reds players. We had so much fun that day! When I looked back on the pictures from our outing, I noticed that my tummy was slightly poked out, but I had no idea at the time that a little person was growing in there.

That Christmas had to have been one of the best ever. We were surrounded by our family, there was love in the air, and we were going to be parents in nine short months.

The following week, we had our first sonogram appointment. When I told my doctor how I had taken three birth control pills after deciding to stop taking them and then the pregnancy tests came back positive, she sent me to have a dating sonogram, just to see how far along in the pregnancy I actually was.

As Chris and I sat out in the waiting area, I flipped through a few of the catalogs on the waiting room table. "Hey, babe," I nudged him, "I think I'd like us to get one of these cribs." I pointed to a convertible crib in the booklet. I remember how when my sister-in-law was pregnant with our niece, she picked out a convertible crib because it could accommodate a growing child. It made sense to me then as an expectant aunt, and it definitely made sense to me now as an expectant mother. "I like that idea," Chris said. As the sonographer called us back to the examination room, I thought "Wow, we're going to buy baby stuff one day!"

+ + +

The sonographer rubbed the scanning tool over my belly and took measurements. She took a few clicks and came back with some interesting news. "There's definitely a baby in there," she said, using the tool. "It looks like you're seven weeks pregnant. So, based on these measurements and the date of your last cycle, it looks like you got pregnant on November 9," she said.

"November 9?" I questioned her.

"Yes, Sunday, November 9, is the day that you conceived," she said.

"That's crazy. On November 10, Chris was in a horrible car accident and it's a miracle that he's alive," I told her, with him sitting next to me. The thought came to me, *My husband survived that car accident because he had a baby on the way.*

With my mind still in a bit of awe over the fact that we got pregnant the day before the accident, the sonographer said, "Your due date is August 16." Wow, we had a little more than eight months to get ready. We were having a baby in August.

As we drove away from the medical center, Chris mentioned that he wanted to go to a nearby clothing and furniture store. As we walked into the store, he asked the salesperson to show him where the baby furniture was. I thought it was odd that he wanted us to look at baby furniture now. I mean, we'd just left our first sonogram appointment, but whatever, we could get an early start on picking out baby stuff.

The salesperson led us back to the baby section and we started looking at all of the different furniture. Chris pointed out a convertible crib, almost like the one we'd seen in the catalog at the doctor's office. "I want to buy one of those," he told the salesperson.

"Babe, are you sure?" I asked him.

"Yes, we're having a baby and the baby has to have a place to sleep," he said.

"But we're only seven weeks pregnant," I told him.

"What does that have to do with anything? We've got a baby coming and the baby has to have a place to sleep!" he said.

I told him okay as the cashier rang up the first purchase of many for our baby.

Over the next week, in addition to buying the crib, Chris went to the store by himself and picked out and bought our baby's Pack

N' Play, car seat, stroller, and swing. He also got a nationally known early-reading program for kids, because, according to him, "Our baby isn't going to be dumb," and he bought a nationally known foreign language program that he said all three of us were going to listen to and learn how to speak Spanish. Evidently, we were all going to be bilingual. Chris was serious about his kid, and he was leaving me in the dust when it came to baby prepping. I was still stuck on the fact that we were pregnant, and here Chris was ready to potty train our eight-week-old gestational seed.

He asked his brother to come over one day to help him take the crib upstairs, but the other baby stuff still took up our living room space.

"Babe, what are we supposed to do with the rest of this stuff?" I asked him one day.

"Well, you're going to clean out your office upstairs and make room for it, because that's going to be the baby's room," he informed me nonchalantly.

When we moved into the three-bedroom townhome a year and a half ago, we'd decided that one of our three bedrooms would be used for sleeping, one of them would be used for Chris's office and photography equipment, and the other room would be used for my office. We had decided that whenever we got pregnant, my office space would be turned into a room for the baby. And according to my husband, it was time for me to clear my office out.

That weekend, I started to notice that I was bleeding a little, and I had no idea why. I called the emergency line to the doctor's office, and when I explained my symptoms to one of the doctors, she callously told me I could possibly be miscarrying. My heart sank. I told her about my symptoms, and she told me to take it easy and she'd have another doctor who actually worked in the OB/GYN office give me a call. When that doctor called me and we talked about my symptoms, he told me the bleeding I was experiencing was normal and that if it would make me feel better, I could take it easy for the rest of the night. I wasn't quite sure what to do—but the thought of taking it easy did make my mind stop racing, so I decided to spend the night in bed watching movies. Besides, with what my husband was telling me, I had my work cut out for me. I had a whole room that had to be cleaned out only to be filled up again with a ton of baby stuff!

WINTER

"When it snows, you have two choices:
shovel or make snow angels."
—Anonymous

CHAPTER NINE

Two weeks after Christmas, as Chris and I stood in line to pay for a car tire, and one week after he'd bought all of our baby's furniture, his phone rang. It was his new job calling. He was supposed to work there for thirty days as a temporary employee and then be hired on full time, but they were calling to say they didn't have enough work for him. Once again, Chris didn't have a job.

After we paid and stepped outside, I could hear Chris on the phone. "Well, what happened? I don't understand. Why did they hire me if they didn't have enough work for me? Do you know what happened?" he asked the account executive representative at the temporary agency where he'd found the job. "Well, okay," I heard him say after a few minutes. He hung up the phone and looked down. "I don't know what happened," he said. Honestly, I didn't either. He had to be at work every morning at 6:30, and Chris always arrived early. He stayed late and didn't have too many complaints about the work he was doing.

I took a deep breath before I responded. I knew that as his wife, my next words could either make or break the situation. "We've been here before, and it's going to be okay," I told him. I took a deep breath of the cold winter air, and we got in the car to get something to eat.

+ + +

Now, Chris and I both were regretting him leaving the job that he had had for all of those years when we first met. He hadn't been in love with the job, but it was stable. It paid good money and we could actually plan our finances. We didn't have to use credit cards to pay for simple things like gas and groceries, and when he worked there, he came home happy. He had been there for ten years and had risen to the rank of assistant supervisor, which he was quite proud of. And at this point, over the last two and a half years, he had gone from not working for eighteen months, to applying for every single job that he could possibly find, to working at a bank where his coworkers told him he moved too slowly and where he wasn't confident, to working at a job where after thirty days, he was told he wasn't needed. He had thought about going back to the original job, but his position didn't exist any longer and there weren't any other positions open in the company.

But me being pregnant and him not having a job did not sit well with him at all. "We have a baby on the way. I have to work," he said.

And I assured him, "You will. Maybe that just wasn't the job for you." I was trying to stay calm, but I knew we were not in a good situation.

"Well, at least I already bought all of the baby's furniture," he said.

"You're right," I said, with a slight smile.

Chris and I had always managed to see the big picture, but we each did so in our own way. Where he saw the big picture and took it all in at once, I saw the big picture and took it in as tiny chunks. Chris saw our baby coming, and as a husband and a father, he wanted to provide everything he could think of that his child would need. I saw our baby coming and knew we'd need to purchase a million and one items but knew we could do it over time. But I was so grateful that in this case, my husband's "big picture, get it done now" attitude had prevailed. We wouldn't have to worry about where money was going to come from in order to pay for our baby's items, because my baby's father had already made the decision to get everything big that he or she would need. I loved Chris as my husband, as my friend, and as my brother in Christ, but with this baby, I was falling in love with my husband as a father. And that felt good.

+ + +

"All right," the doctor said, "Are you ready to hear the baby's heartbeat?"

"We get to hear it today?" I asked with excitement. I was only ten weeks pregnant, and I thought I needed to be further along before we could hear the little thumping of the baby's heart.

"Yeah, you get to hear it today," the doctor said, smiling back. All of this baby stuff had me in awe. I was starting to gain weight, and for the first time in my life I didn't care about the extra pounds. Anything for our baby. And now we were going to hear his or her heartbeat. This was all so exciting. "Okay, lie back on the table and I'm going to put this little monitor up to your stomach and you'll be able to hear the heartbeat." I had Chris grab my phone so he could record my reaction to hearing the baby's heartbeat for the first time.

As the doctor put the monitor to my stomach, we heard a fast and loud thump that was the most amazing sound I'd had ever heard. "Wowwwww," I said, as I felt my eyes widen in amazement. "Do you hear it? Do you hear it?" I asked Chris excitedly.

"Yeah, I hear it," he said back, smiling. "That's the sound of a healthy baby," he said with wonder and fact in his voice.

We sat in awe and the doctor smiled. "Yep, that's a healthy heartbeat," she said.

We left the hospital that day smiling. Seeing all of the baby items in our home and my little belly starting to show, combined with us hearing the heartbeat, made this pregnancy seem more and more real by the day. We were having a baby.

+ + +

Thankfully, within a month of losing his job, Chris was able to secure employment through a temporary agency, where he would be working for a large and well-known international consumer company. His role would be data-focused and since he loved numbers, we figured it would be a good fit. Right before Valentine's Day, when I was eleven weeks along, I'd shared our pregnancy with my coworkers. At the end of one of my small team meetings, I announced, "We're going to have a brand new team member joining us in August. Guess what? I'm knocked up!" I didn't care that the real meaning of "knocked up" had a somewhat bad connotation to it; I thought it was funny and they'd know exactly what I was saying.

After the meeting was over, I shared the same phrase with my other coworkers, and their expressions were priceless. They were all excited and happy. I'd started my job right out of college as a fresh-faced, twenty-two-year-old who had CEO-like dreams, and in many ways, I'd grown up in the department of the hospital where I worked. My coworkers had become more like family members to me throughout the years, and all of us really cared about each other. We really enjoyed the work we did, and we also enjoyed each other. I was blessed to work in a department where, for the most part and on most days, everyone got along. There was nothing like it. I'd always said if I was going to spend eight hours a day with the same group of people that I wanted to make sure I liked them, and I really, really liked my coworkers. A few of them gave me big hugs in addition to the excited expressions on their faces. Some of the more seasoned people in the department had watched me grow from a young lady who was bright-eyed and bushy-tailed to a woman who was dating the guy of her dreams, a beautiful bride, and now a future mom. They were excited for me, and I appreciated them sharing my joy.

To make matters more fun, the running joke was that there were always three people pregnant in our department. And not to my surprise, our baby would have two other playmates. Two women in my department were pregnant, plus two of the young women in another department on the same floor were pregnant, plus five more in the building that I worked in. Our baby was going to grow up with all types of friends at his or her mommy's job, and I couldn't have been happier.

+ + +

One winter day, I came home to a piece of mail addressed to me from a law firm. I had no idea what it could be, but when I opened it and read through it, my mouth dropped. I was being sued. I stood still in the middle of the living room floor trying to figure out who was suing me and for what.

I quickly thought about what I could've done to be sued. I was a law-abiding citizen. I didn't do anything that wrong...well, except for speeding. I did drive fast, but I had been caught driving fast only a few times, which resulted in three official speeding tickets, which were all paid. So, what in the world did I do—or not do—to get sued? My eyes scanned the letter, and it hit me like a ton of bricks: We hadn't paid the credit card bill Chris and I had racked up a year and a half earlier when he initially lost his job. We'd said we'd pay the bill when we had the money to pay it, but instead of at least paying the minimum amount, we had opted to stop paying it until we could.

Our plan seemed like a good one at the time, but as I stood there with the letter in my hand, I knew it wasn't a good choice.

"Babe, they're suing us for almost $10,000," I told Chris.

"But we didn't pile up $10,000 worth of debt on that card," he responded.

"I know. I mean, we did accumulate about $4,500, but we definitely didn't accumulate $10,000," I told him. "And we don't have it to give them." Heck, if we'd had $10,000, we would've originally given them the $4,500 that we actually spent! Didn't lawsuits go on a record? What in the world were we going to do? Chris had just started his new job, we had a baby on the way, and I wasn't making enough to pay off a $10,000 credit card bill.

"All right, don't panic," Chris said.

Of the two of us, he was the calm one. Sometimes that trait irked me about him. There were days when I wanted him to be more emotional about our circumstances—but that wasn't him. He was as cool as a cucumber, and I was as hot as a tamale. And maybe that's why we balanced each other out so well. I could be calm, but this was not the time to be calm! I was being sued for money that I didn't have and for money that, truthfully, I hadn't even spent. As I flipped through the accompanying documents for the lawsuit, it eventually dawned on me that the interest rate on the card in addition to the late fees that had accumulated was where the credit card company got their $10,000 figure. I had heard of other people getting sued for debt and for a lot more than $10,000, but to us $10,000 was a lot. Plus, we had a baby on the way. That night, I felt defeated. I didn't know what to do.

+ + +

Over the next week, I started getting postcards in the mail from lawyers all over town who said they wanted to take on my case. *Great,*

I thought, *I'm being branded as a person who doesn't pay her bills.* And the messed-up thing about it was I *was* actually a person who hadn't paid her bills, which was why I was getting sued! But didn't they know that my husband had lost his job for eighteen months, and didn't they know we had other stuff we needed to pay for? And didn't they know we had a baby on the way? I guess none of those things mattered because we hadn't done what we were supposed to do.

All through college and into adulthood, I had prided myself on paying my bills on time and keeping an eye on every penny that came in and went out of my account. When Chris and I got married and joined our money together, I did the same. But with all of our bills starting to add up, plus everything else that was going on in our lives, I hadn't been doing such a great job of keeping a close eye on our finances, and that relaxed attitude was now proving to be detrimental to us.

To add insult to injury, the week after I received the lawsuit letter, I got a certified letter in the mail letting me know our medical practice was dropping me as a patient. The letter read that I hadn't paid my current medical bill and if it weren't paid within a short amount of time, the practice would dismiss me. If I thought I was defeated before, I was even more defeated now. I had just paid one of our medical bills two weeks prior. And I had paid over $300. To me, on our minimal budget, I thought that was a lot. Surely the letter was sent to us by mistake. I couldn't understand why our practice would be dropping me. And in my mind, if they were dropping me, they were probably dropping Chris, too. I was four months pregnant and my husband was receiving MS treatment and care from a doctor's team at the practice. I had been a patient there for almost nine years. So, here we were with a lawsuit and we were being dropped from the medical practice. The sad part was we still didn't have money to pay these amounts being demanded of us.

That day, as I was going to meet a friend, I drove alongside a river, and a quick thought came to me: *I could just drive off into the river and it could all be over.* But as quickly as the thought came, it was as if I could hear my unborn child's voice in my head saying, "Keep on fighting, Mommy. It's gonna be okay." A tear trailed down my face and I snapped back into reality. I didn't really want to end my life; I just wanted all of this bad stuff to stop happening.

The lawsuit had shaken me up. I had been in minor trouble before just like everyone else at some point. In high school, I had gone to an amusement park with some friends and skipped going to work, so I'd gotten in trouble with my boss. I'd always had a bit of a sassy mouth on me, and when I had too much attitude with my parents, they put me back in my place. Other than that, I had done the best I could to live a life in which I stayed out of trouble. I was the girl who cried when she got her name put on the board in kindergarten and in second grade for talking too much (surprise!). My parents had taught me early on about cause and effect, choices and consequences. I'd always done my best to make sure that my choices were good so that my consequences wouldn't be bad. And here lately, a few of my choices hadn't been that great, and the consequences were starting to add up against me. That just didn't feel good.

On the following Monday, I called my doctor's billing office as soon as it opened so I could figure out why we were being dropped from the practice. And as I'd thought, there was a misunderstanding. Due to all of the different appointments that led to the breast surgery, I had accumulated three different bills with three different departments at the medical center where the doctor's practice was located. I complained to the billing lady that I had just paid money a few weeks prior and that the practice should streamline its bills so as to not confuse their patients. Although I'd paid $300 to one department, I still had an outstanding bill with another department. She assured me I wasn't the only person who had complained about needing a better billing process. As she read me my confirmation number, she told me I would be reinstated as a patient immediately, and I let out a breath of relief. If there was one thing we needed right now, it was medical care. I had never been so happy to pay a bill in my life.

With the medical practice issue behind us, I needed to focus on whatever was going to happen with the lawsuit. After responding to a card from one of the lawyers I didn't know, consulting with my lawyer friends, and looking up some information online, we decided to try to fight the case, with me representing myself. As a little girl, one of the many things I had said I wanted to be when I grew up was a lawyer. I didn't think I'd actually end up being my own.

When it was time for my case to begin, I stepped up to the lectern marked for the defendant and pled my case. I'd gotten some help from my lawyer friends on what to say and how to defend myself. I never denied that the debt was mine, but I didn't admit to it either. Before it was time for the opposing lawyer and me to leave the courtroom, the judge said she would be setting up our next court date.

What? I thought to myself. Another court date was not in my plans. And when she said the court date would be on June 15, I spoke into the microphone "Your honor, I'll be exactly seven months pregnant on June 15." I figured June 15 was close enough to June 16 for me to make my "exact" claim. "And coming back to court is going to be an extremely stressful situation, and I know that if I'm stressed, my unborn child will feel that stress, and that won't be good for either of us." I went on, "And because I'll be seven months pregnant, my baby could come early, so unless someone is prepared to deliver an early baby while I'm in court in June, I don't think we should come back to court on that day." I rested my case.

I had been told by my lawyer friends that I should try to settle the court case with the opposing lawyer, and the little bun in my oven was a good enough reason for me to get my pregnant self out of the courtroom and to do my best to settle. "I understand, Mrs. Jones," the judge said. "Why don't you and opposing counsel meet over in the corner and see if the two of you can figure something out." I breathed a sigh of relief. I wasn't sure what was to come, but at that point, anything was better than me having to come back to court. Sheesh.

I stepped over to the corner and the opposing lawyer approached me. "Mrs. Jones," he said, "why don't you take my card so we can try to work this out." I took his card, promised to be in touch, and left the courtroom. I never, ever wanted to be there again. Over the next several weeks, the lawyer told me to send him a list of all of the hardships Chris and I had been through over the last couple of years and asked me to explain all of our financial obligations that had prevented us from paying our credit card bill.

After he received the list and he and I corresponded, one of the first things he said to me was, "Mrs. Jones, I am so sorry that you and your husband have been and are going through so much." I figured my life had to have been pretty messed up for an opposing lawyer to feel sorry for me. We eventually settled out of court for an amount Chris and I could actually afford to pay. I was happy to have the court case behind me, and I promised myself that I would never be in that situation again.

CHAPTER TEN

Chris and I had been waiting for April 3, 2015, to come since the day we found out we were pregnant. Was this little person a boy or a girl? We had agreed that if we had a little boy, he would be named after his dad, Christopher Louis Jones. Chris had always wanted a junior, specifically so he could call the baby Junior and refer to himself as Senior. Meanwhile, everyone else and I had decided that if the baby were a boy, we'd call him CJ, as in Christopher Junior. And if we were having a little girl, her name would be Arielle Nicole Jones. Nicole is my middle name, and we thought it was good enough to use again for our little princess. Would we be cheering for team pink or team blue? Would I be a Girl Scout troop leader (again), or would I be a football mom who brought snacks for my team of boys? Would Chris have a little buddy to play football with, or would he be introduced to the world of dolls and tea parties? April 3 was game day, and we were excited.

We got to the doctor's office early, eager to find out what we were having, as were our family, friends, and coworkers. Our appointment was at 8:30 that morning. That way, we'd both be able to get to work before lunchtime.

We walked into the same room where we had our first sonogram. As usual, Chris joked with the sonographer as I hopped up on the table. "I will love you forever if you tell me I'm having a boy," Chris told the sonographer as she and I both laughed. Chris wanted this baby to be a boy, and he did not hide it. When people would ask me what we wanted to have, I would say the same thing every single time: "I want a healthy baby." Having worked at a children's hospital, I'd seen babies and children who lived with severe medical issues. It didn't really matter to me the sex of the baby. I just wanted the baby to be healthy. Chris was a different story. When people asked him what he wanted, he quickly told them his answer. "A boy," he'd say, almost sticking his chest out. He said it with such conviction, it was as if he knew what we were having before the baby was born. "We are having a boy," he would tell me. And if I joked around with him and even hinted that we could possibly be having a girl, he got upset. One time, he got so mad that he stormed out of the room. He told me that his only dream in life was to have a little boy, and by me telling him otherwise, I was going against his dream. I didn't mean anything by it. I just thought it was funny to joke about it, but Chris didn't see it that way. I wondered how someone who had once said that he would be perfectly fine if we didn't have any kids could be so sure that we were going to have a boy. So here we were—the day of truth—finding out what we were having. Or I should say, I and everyone else were finding out what we were having. In my husband's mind, he already knew.

As I lay on the table in the dimly lit room, Chris and I stared at the large screen ahead of me where we could see everything the sonographer could see. Our baby, who showed up as a neon light blue on the screen, looked larger than life. The sonographer was silent as she rubbed the sonogram tool over my stomach. "Wow, he has a big head!" I said, laughing, as Chris and I both said in unison, "That comes from your family!"

As the sonographer moved down, she stopped quite a few times to take a variety of different pictures. We thought it was completely normal. After all, one of my coworkers who was also pregnant had prepared me for our gender-reveal day. She told me that at that point, the appointment was more than the doctor just telling us what the sex of the baby was. She told me the doctor would look at the baby's organs and how fast he or she was growing. My coworker and I were only three months apart in our pregnancies, and having her to talk to had been fun along the way. For some reason, we would always end up at the bathroom and the water fountain at the same time, along with the other three pregnant women on our floor. On any given day, it would look like a pregnant lady party in the hallway. My coworker and her husband weren't finding out what they were having, but Chris and I definitely wanted to find out. Her conversation with me about how detailed the gender scan appointment was helped convince me that I shouldn't have it done until I was at least twenty weeks pregnant to be sure the baby was developed enough so the doctor could see all of his or her organs very clearly. So, here we were at twenty weeks and six days, looking at all of our baby's limbs, organs, and everything else, anxiously waiting to learn what we were having.

"Are you ready to find out what you're having?" the sonographer asked Chris and me.

"Yeah," I said, smiling.

"I already know we're having a boy," Chris said confidently through a big smile.

After me doing a few wiggles and the sonographer pressing on my belly to get the baby to move around, I saw what she was looking at and she announced it, "You're having a boy!"

"Really?" Chris asked. "We're really having a boy?" he said, getting up out of his seat.

"Yes, you're having a boy," the sonographer said again.

"Yeah, I can definitely tell that's a little boy," I said, looking at the little organ protruding between my son's legs.

"Yeah, I'm having a boy! That's my boy!" Chris exclaimed loudly. "I'm having a boy!" And then, as promised, he turned to the sonographer and said, "I love you," as all three of us laughed.

The sonographer continued her scan as it sank in. *We're having a little boy,* I thought to myself. It was going to be fun having Chris and a mini-Chris running around our home. I knew we'd be laughing even more when the baby was born than we did now.

"Wow, his stomach is really big," I said matter-of-factly. "He's definitely a boy," I concluded from my observation.

"Yeah, that's my boy! That just means that he's eating real good!" Chris said.

"Yep!" I agreed. The sonographer continued to rub the tool over my stomach for a few more minutes and explained that a doctor would be coming in to speak with us. "Okay, that sounds good," I told her as Chris nodded his head in agreement.

When the sonographer left the room, Chris continued to tell me, "I knew it; I knew it. I knew we were having a boy. All of you were against me, but I knew we were having a boy." No one disputed Chris's thoughts per se; it was just that he was more adamant about his conviction of us having a boy than anyone else. Everyone else was up in the air over the gender of the baby, and because my stomach had grown so fast so quickly, a few people even told us that they thought we'd be having twins. But the entire pregnancy, Chris assured me that there was only one child growing inside of me and that one child was a boy. And on this day, in the sonographer's office, he was proven right.

As we waited for the doctor to come into the room, Chris called his oldest brother. Of his three older brothers, he was the one Chris was closest to, and he spoke with him several times every week. Because Chris had lived with him and his wife before we had gotten married, he and Chris shared a special bond. And his brother and his wife were like a big brother and sister to me, too. We were very close to their two young daughters and they were all looking forward to finding out what we were having. "Hey, bruh, what's up? It's a boy! Yeah, it's definitely a boy! I tried to tell everybody we were having a boy," Chris exclaimed on the phone. When Chris finished talking to his brother, he called my brother, almost starting the conversation the same exact way: "What's up, bruh? It's Chris! We found out we're having a boy! Yep, it's a boy!" My husband was super-excited and I was happy for him.

While he made calls to the future uncles, I figured I could sneak in a couple of calls to my family. "Mom, we know what we're having," I said with a slyness in my tone.

"Okay, what is it?" she asked with anticipation.

"It's a boy," I said grinning. "It's a boy, Mommy; the baby is a boy!" I heard her telling her mother in the background.

When I got off the phone with her, I called my dad. "What's up, baby girl?" my dad asked.

"All right, we know what we're having," I told him.

"What is it?" he asked.

"It's a boy," I told him.

"Wowwww," he said, using one of his expressive signature phrases that I, too, often used. "I'm gonna have a grandson."

"Yep, you're going to have a grandson," I told him, smiling. My dad had been one of the people who was strongly pulling for the baby to be a little girl, but it didn't really matter to him. He was just excited to be a grandparent. As I was wrapping up my short conversation with him, the doctor walked into the room.

"Okay, Daddy. I've got to go, the doctor's walking in to talk with us," I told him as we hung up.

The doctor walked over toward me in her white lab coat, and I noticed that her face was almost devoid of color. She pulled up a swivel chair next to me and looked at me with downcast eyes, saying, "Mrs. Jones, I hate to tell you this, but your baby has multiple abnormalities." I sat frozen as the words came out of her mouth and my world stopped.

My immediate response to her was, "You're kidding, right?" She had to be kidding. This must be some kind of joke that doctors pull on expecting parents to ease them into the idea of having a baby. She couldn't be telling us the truth. With my eyes locked on hers, I expected her to tell me she was kidding and that we could go home. But instead she gave me another answer.

"I'm sorry. I'm not. Your baby has multiple issues," she said flatly and hopelessly. She was noticeably affected by whatever she had seen on our sonogram results. She even looked like she wanted her response to us to be different.

"Okay, well, we're fine," I told her, in response to her comment about the baby having multiple issues.

And she responded, "But I'm not."

I looked at her again with a stern look and told her, "But I need you to be, because we are."

Chris captured her attention from the other side of the room, "What types of abnormalities are you talking about?" he asked.

"Well, let me show you," she said as she rubbed more gel over my stomach and started to press on my belly with the sonogram tool. She waved the sonogram wand over our little boy from the top of his head to the bottom of his feet. "Well, the baby's head is big and it looks like his hands have something going on with them. They look like they're balled up in little fists, and his wrists look like they may be clubbed." She continued: "Something is going on with his umbilical cord. And his feet look like they're clubbed also."

Chris and I looked at the screen and we still didn't know what exactly she was talking about. This was our first child. We didn't know what a normal, healthy baby's sonogram was supposed to look like; we had to go with what the doctor was telling us.

She then said, "Based on these issues, I think he has a chromosomal disorder. And the only way that we are going to find out what exactly is wrong is if we run some additional tests on him." She then recommended that we get an amniocentesis, a procedure in which a doctor inserts a long needle into a woman's womb to extract fluid from around the fetus. The fluid can then give doctors clues and answers regarding the baby's possible medical conditions. We'd been given the option of having an amniocentesis done before, but we agreed not to do it. I had heard the procedure could be a little costly, and we definitely didn't want to incur any additional costs we didn't need to have. And even more importantly, we had agreed that whether the baby had issues or not, we were going to love it. The results of an amniocentesis weren't going to change that stance for us, so we had opted not to have it done.

The doctor went on, "Based on what I'm seeing, I think he has a chromosome disorder known as Trisomy 18. It is a fatal medical diagnosis, and often times when parents receive this type of diagnosis, they decide to terminate."

As quickly as she could get it out of her mouth, I responded, "That's not an option for us, so we need some other options." How dare she suggest that we terminate our child? By this time, I had started to feel him kick and twist and turn inside of me. We had heard his heart beat. In our minds, he was as alive as we were. Ending his life because he had a few medical issues didn't even cross our minds. I had heard of women who had to make the sad choice of terminating their baby because the baby being born would have caused the mother serious harm or could have caused her death. But this was not that. The doctor told us the baby had issues, not that I was going to die if we continued the pregnancy. I was upset that she would even bring that up.

Chris spoke up, "So what are our other options? Because we are not terminating our child."

"Well, you have a few options. You could get a blood test, but if all of your blood work comes back normal, we'll be at the same place we are now and you'd need to get an amniocentesis to learn more about what could possibly be going on with the baby."

"Well, I'm sure my blood work is going to come back normal," I said.

She responded with, "I suggest you have the amniocentesis and then we go from there. We'll see what those results produce, and then we'll at least have a better idea of what is going on."

"Is that what the best option is?" Chris asked, sounding a little worried.

The doctor said to me, "If you were my sister, I would recommend that you have the amnio."

"Okay, then I guess we'll have it done," I said, numb to my core, trying to comprehend everything that was happening.

We had come to the doctor's office to find out the gender of our child, not to be told he had medical issues. Not to run any tests on him or me. Not to be left feeling like our world was being turned upside down for what felt like the millionth time within the last two years. Why was this happening? And why was it happening to us? I rarely drank, and Chris didn't drink at all. We didn't smoke. We were never exposed to illegal substances or recreational drugs, so why in the world, how in the world, was the baby growing inside of me having issues?

The doctor told Chris and me that she was going to let us talk for a moment while she got the materials needed to perform the amniocentesis.

Chris slid his chair over next to me and tears began to well up in my eyes as he took my hands into his. "Babe, it's going to be okay," he assured me. "You didn't do anything to cause this, okay?"

I nodded and the tears began to fall.

"Dear Lord," he started praying, and we both nodded our heads. "Please watch over my wife and watch over my baby. Lord, we know what the doctor is saying, but God we believe in You and we believe that our son is healthy. Jesus, let the results of the tests come back completely normal," he said fervently. "Jesus, thank You for my boy, and thank You that my boy is healthy. In Jesus's name, we pray. Amen." Chris ended right as the doctor came back into the room.

I was still trying to gather my thoughts as she walked over to me with a tray of medical materials. "I need to go to the bathroom," I quietly said. All pregnant women needed to go to the bathroom several times a day, so my excuse to get out of the room didn't seem like it was anything more than me just announcing that I had to go pee.

"Sure," the doctor said. "As soon as you leave this room, it'll be to your left. When you come back, we'll perform the test."

I held in my tears and every ounce of emotion that I was feeling and almost ran to the bathroom. With one swift move, I opened and closed the bathroom door, locked it, and fell to my knees. I was bent over with my hands spread out to hold me up, and my tears began to flow and hit the floor. I prayed harder than I had ever prayed before. I didn't know what else to do. There wasn't anything else I could do. There was nothing else Chris could do. And based on what the doctor was saying, there was nothing else she could do. All I knew to do was to literally cry out to Jesus. I believed in the power of prayer. I had lived my life believing in the power of prayer. Chris and I believed that God had the authority to change our circumstance at any given time, and while we weren't in control, we knew who was. And we knew Him. We had relationships with Him, individually and collectively. I didn't believe God had allowed my husband to survive a major car crash only to allow our child to be born with medical issues that were serious enough for a doctor to suggest termination. I didn't believe that a God who loved us through all of the ups and downs of the past two years would allow our child's life to be in jeopardy. I could not fathom that the same God who had proven Himself faithful to us every single day would allow this—whatever this was—to happen to us. Not the God that we served and knew. Not the God who controlled the universe. Not the God that had created everything in the world and had graciously allowed us to live in it. That wasn't the God we knew. Why was this happening to us? If my tears could've stained the gray tile, they would have on that day. When I prayed, I believed the words that I was praying, and on that day, in that bathroom, right outside of the sonography room, I prayed and believed that our child would be born healthy.

I gathered myself and went back into the room and hopped back on the table. I had gathered resolve and faith in the bathroom. I had gathered composure, and though the circumstances before us seemed insurmountable, I was ready to fight for the life of our child.

I lay back on the table and the doctor explained to us what was going to happen during the procedure. Chris and I listened intently. The doctor explained that the needle would go through my stomach and into my uterus and a small amount of fluid would be taken from around the baby. As she inserted the needle carefully, Chris and I watched the screen. We saw the needle go into the sac of fluid that our son was in. I, already being an over cautious and protective mother, spoke to the baby. "Little boy, I don't want you to get poked by the needle. Mama doesn't want you to get poked," I calmly said as I saw the needle nearing the baby's head. I figured that since we knew the baby was a boy, I could start speaking to him as our son. And then, as if he'd heard me, we watched his hands come together and shield his face. "Wow," I spoke up. His actions let me know he could hear us and that this foreign needle was invading his space. He didn't want it there, and neither did Chris or I. But we knew it needed to be done.

When the doctor was finished, she told us they would have answers for us as soon as possible, and that for the rest of the day, I should go home and rest. When we asked her what types of tests they were going to do, she told us a FISH (fluorescence in situ hybridization), a karyotype, and a microarray. She told us that if the FISH came back normal, the doctors would run a karyotype, and if that came back normal, the doctors would run a microarray. She and her team were determined to get some answers about our baby.

She explained the tests to us at a very high medical level and then explained them to us in layman's terms to make sure we understood. A FISH would consist of the doctors looking at our son's chromosomes to make sure all of them were there. It would be like a person looking at a bookshelf to make sure every book that was supposed to be there, was. The karyotype would look at the chromosomes' size, shape, and number. It would be like looking at all of the books on the bookshelf to make sure the right titles were in the proper order. And the microarray would be the doctors looking at all of the baby's chromosomes to make sure they were intact, as if a person inspected the pages in all of the books on a bookshelf.

After the doctor finished with the amniocentesis and I got dressed, I asked the sonographer to snap a picture of us. That was the plan before the doctor's report of the baby having issues, and there was no need to change the plan now. We were still excited that we were becoming first-time parents to a little boy, so we weren't going to let the doctor's report rob us of those joys. I handed my camera phone to the sonographer, and before she snapped the picture, she said, "I'm so sorry all of this is going on. I'm not allowed to say what I see. Only the doctors can do that."

Her words explained why she didn't have a big response when Chris and I were pointing out that our son's head and stomach were big. Of all of the babies she had seen, she could tell when something was "off," and she knew that our baby had issues but she wasn't allowed to say that to us.

"It's okay. You were doing your job," I told her.

"Yeah, it's okay," Chris said. "I still love you for telling me I'm having a boy." That made her laugh. She snapped a few pictures, and we walked out of the room.

After we left the medical center, I called my parents back and shared with them that the doctors had some concerns about the baby, but I was steadfast in also saying he would be fine. My parents listened, but they were definitely concerned about our circumstances. On the inside, I was heartbroken and didn't know what to do. I cried a lot that day. I was just trying to make sense of what was going on. Chris, on the other hand, was fine. He went to work while I obeyed the doctor's orders and stayed home to rest. Chris's day was normal, because for him, he never believed that anything was wrong with the baby. It was as if the doctors were trying to get him to understand and believe something he refused to believe.

The next day we went to a church festival that was in preparation for Easter Sunday. While at the carnival, one of my friends from church shared with me that she was pregnant too, and I was super excited for her, while nervous for us. In fact, at that point, several of us young women at church were expecting babies. There were so many of us that the pastor joked with us and said we'd have to build a bigger nursery to accommodate all of the new babies that were coming. And none of us minded one bit.

Many of us were even due within days or weeks of each other. One of the girls was due the same day as we were, and another was due two days after that. Even with our sad doctor's appointment the day prior, I still believed in my heart that all of us at church would have healthy babies. Our babies would grow up together and have fun with each other and have play dates. Just like all of the babies that were on their way at work. There was no way that any of them, ours included, wouldn't actually make it to this life or that he or she would have medical issues and problems.

At the carnival, I walked around and saw all of the other expectant mommies and laughed and chatted with them, holding on to the secret deep within that the doctor said our baby had serious medical issues. Everyone else was happy about the pending arrival of their child, so I thought I should be. We were the first in the bunch of pregnant couples who found out the gender of our baby, so while I revealed that we were having a boy, I didn't say he had received a bad doctor's report. But a few women I was close to, who already had had children, could detect the sadness in my voice and see the worry behind my smile. I shared with them what the doctor had said and how our appointment had gone, and the women hugged me and told me they would pray for us. One couple in particular assured us that everything would be fine. The husband even said that doctors had told him that three of his five children were supposed to be born with medical issues, but all five of them were healthy kids. In fact, the more couples we talked to, the more we learned that many of them had received disheartening medical diagnoses for their children, but nonetheless, they had given birth to completely fine children. That made us feel better. We started to gain confidence that maybe the doctors weren't correct. Maybe they just thought they were seeing something. After all, we trusted God that our child would be fine. My mantra became, "Doctors practice medicine, but we know the Creator of it." I was taking the stance that even though the doctors said what they said, Chris and I knew God, and we had such a relationship with Him that at any given time, He could intervene and turn our situation around.

After we returned home from the carnival, the doctor called to let us know we had our first batch of test results back. She told us our son hadn't tested positive for Trisomy 13, Trisomy 18 (better known as Edwards syndrome), or Trisomy 21 (better known as Down syndrome). That was the best news we'd received all day. She told us the doctors would then run the karyotype test. Because the first test hadn't been positive, we felt confident that the second test would be negative too.

That Easter Sunday, I went to church and praised God and sang along with the choir. I knew it was always easy to praise God when things are going well, but it's during the tough times when a person's faith is truly tested. This would just be a tough time for Chris and me, just like so many times before. But that didn't mean we would stop having faith or stop praising God. This was the perfect time for us to believe in His miracle-providing power.

CHAPTER ELEVEN

The next morning, we had a follow-up appointment with another doctor in the practice. She'd received our test results and our son's prognosis from the Friday before. She told us she was sorry for everything we were going through. She also told us that from that point on, our pregnancy would be considered "high risk" and she would be referring us to the larger medical center near downtown. I had hoped I'd be able to deliver our baby in the medical center where we had been going to have all our appointments. That hospital was planning to open a birthing center within the next week, and I wanted our baby to be one of the first born there. But the high-risk diagnosis meant I would need to continue my pregnancy at a better-equipped facility that could handle emergency deliveries and medical issues for moms and babies, if needed.

"Mrs. Jones, you won't be able to have this baby here," the doctor told me. "Maybe the next one you will, though."

I wasn't even focused on the "next one." According to Chris, this was going to be "the only one," and after all of this news, I was almost on board with him on that.

I asked the doctor a very practical question: "Should we still have a baby shower?" In my mind, even if the baby were going to be born with issues, he would still need clothes and bottles and other stuff that people brought to baby showers. But instead of telling me that it was okay for me to go forward with planning a shower, she told me to wait to see what the doctors at the high-risk facility would tell me. At that moment, I knew that whatever "this" was, it was serious. The doctor was telling me not to even have a shower for the baby. How serious were these medical issues our baby was being diagnosed with? The doctor told us to make an appointment with the high-risk practice doctors, and she wished us the best of luck.

When I made the appointment with the high-risk doctors, they informed me that in addition to seeing them, the baby would need to get an in-utero MRI, and I would need to schedule a team meeting with a group of pediatric doctors at the local children's hospital to discuss our baby's issues. It all sounded so overwhelming, but I figured that the doctors knew what was best. So I scheduled all of the appointments and waited for their dates to arrive.

One week after our initial sonographer appointment, the baby had his MRI, and much to my surprise, he flipped, flopped, and jumped around in my stomach more than I had ever felt him before. He twisted and turned, and at the loud knocking sound of the MRI, it felt like he was dancing. I actually got a kick out of our little guy. Surely this baby didn't have anything wrong with him. He was way too active! In our minds, if something were truly wrong with him, he wouldn't have moved around so much. And what about him putting his hands up in front of his face to shield himself from the amniocentesis needle? Surely, if there were something wrong with him, he wouldn't have known to do that. Those doctors just didn't know what they were talking about!

The following Wednesday was our personal "D-day," meaning a day full of meetings with doctors. On that day we'd be seeing at least one high-risk doctor, a genetics counselor and a geneticist, and a team of doctors who would give us more insight about our baby. Such a big schedule for such a little person.

Our appointments started with the high-risk doctor, who happened to be a colleague of the doctor who read our sonogram results. The high-risk doctor examined me and did yet another sonogram on the baby. He waved the wand over my stomach and confirmed that he saw the same issues his colleague had seen only weeks prior. "I think he may have what's called Dandy Walker syndrome," he said.

"What's that?" I asked.

"Well, it's a brain deformity that occurs in an area at the back of the brain in the area that controls movement and cognitive learning. And he may have Joubert syndrome," he said, while waving the wand over the baby's head to get a better look at his brain. "There's also a lot of extra fluid around him," the doctor told us as I lay on the table and Chris sat in the chair next to me. As he continued to move the wand over me, the doctor asked, "Has anyone else in either of your families ever had a baby born with medical issues?"

My mother and I had talked about her road to having children only a few times. I knew that she and my dad had gotten pregnant shortly after they were married, but unfortunately they miscarried the baby. Then they had gotten pregnant with me, and I was born completely healthy. Then, when I was four months old, they had gotten pregnant again. But when it was time for the baby to be born, my mom went beyond her due date, which caused concern for her and the doctors. At an appointment, the doctors told her the baby would be born with medical issues and that he would die shortly thereafter. They didn't know about the baby's medical issues before that appointment, and by that time, there was nothing they could do to help my mom or the baby. With no solution for saving her child, they told her to go home and let nature take its course. About a week later, my mom gave birth to a little boy who had brain abnormalities and a cleft palate. Approximately eight hours later, he passed away.

My parents, a young couple at the time, received family support, but when their son passed away, people didn't openly discuss those types of losses. My parents grieved almost silently and moved on with their lives. And three years later, they had another healthy baby: my younger brother. As I was growing up, no one discussed the baby who died. I believe in my heart that it was too painful for my parents. Plus, with them having my living younger brother, they regained confidence that they could have healthy children. There wasn't a need to resurface such a painful experience if they didn't have to. So they didn't.

When I was eleven, my mom, dad, brother, and I traveled to New York City to visit some long-distance relatives, and that's when I learned about my brother who had died. While catching up and having regular conversation, I overheard one of my older cousins ask my parents how old my brother and I were. They said something to the effect of they knew there was one who had passed away and they were so happy that my parents had another son. The ever-so-attentive girl that I was held on to every word. What other child were my relatives talking about? All my life, I had only known about my younger living brother. For the previous several years, I had been praying to God that He would send me a little sister, even at times pretending that my baby dolls were my younger siblings. But based off what my older cousins were saying, I possibly had one. But where was she? They hadn't specified if this other child was a boy or a girl, so I automatically believed it was a little girl. Why would my parents choose only to keep me and my brother but give this other baby away? Did we have another sibling who my parents had put up for adoption? I had so many questions, and I didn't understand our situation. How could I ask my parents about this other child? Would I get in trouble for listening in on grown folks' conversations?

The rest of our trip and after we got home, my mind kept coming back to my sibling. Finally, when I couldn't take it anymore, I pressed my mother for answers. "Mom, when we were in New York, our cousin said that you and Dad had another baby," I started one evening, while sitting on my parents' bed watching TV with my mom. "Where is the baby? What happened?" My eleven-year-old, inquisitive mind was begging for information. I needed to know what happened to my other sibling.

"Let me show you," my mom said. She got up from where she was sitting and joined me at the foot of the bed. She reached underneath it and pulled out a dark-brown, fireproof lock box with a thick, dark-brown handle. She slowly opened it and explained, "Your dad and I had another baby when you were sixteen months old. He was born, but he didn't survive for long."

I could feel my heart sinking in my chest. I was so young, but I could tell from the tone in my mother's voice that although this was something she and my dad had put behind them, it was a point of sadness for her.

"Mommy, what happened?" I asked, as she began to go through papers and envelopes in the box.

"He was born with part of his brain missing and he had a cleft palate," she told me, pulling out a gold envelope with pictures in it. There she sat with a few Polaroid pictures in her hand of my little brother who had passed away. He looked so precious. His skin was brown, like ours, and he wore a light-blue outfit with a little white hat.

"What was his name, Mommy?" I asked, and she told me. Part of me felt guilty. Even at eleven, I was in tune with my emotions, and at that moment, I felt so bad for asking my mom to tell me about her baby. I then thought about pictures of me from when I was a toddler. I had seen pictures of my mom pregnant when I was only a year old, and it had never quite added up for me. My living brother was three years and nine months younger than me, but in these pictures, my mom was clearly pregnant and I was barely walking. I always wondered about the baby in her stomach. I knew I wasn't the best math student, but her being pregnant when I was that young didn't equate to my living brother being inside of her when I was only sixteen months old. And now I knew. Because I'd asked and wouldn't stop asking, my mom felt like she needed to tell me what happened, and she felt like I was mature enough to handle it. She and I talked a bit longer on that day, and when our conversation was over, it was over. I'd hear about that child only a couple of times more leading to my own pregnancy. Once, a couple of years prior to me getting pregnant, my parents' church asked my mom to give an encouraging speech about how she'd made it through a hard time, and she shared the story of the baby who passed away. The other time was before Chris and I got married. I had a very grown-up, woman-to-woman conversation with Mom about what she and my dad did for birth control. During that conversation, she reminded me that she and my father had conceived four times. But in between the day when I was eleven, when she told me about my brother who passed away, and the day when I was twenty-seven, asking her about birth control options, we didn't really talk about my baby brother.

When people asked my parents how many children they had, they always answered "two," referring to my living brother and me. And they always made it a point to share with others how much they loved us. My dad, many times, added that we were a blessing to him and my mom.

My parents treated my brother and me as though each of us was an only child, even after we became adults. They gave us love and attention and showered us with gifts (when we had earned them), all while disciplining us and making the lines very clear that they were our parents and we were their children. As an adult, I realized one of the reasons why my parents loved us so much was probably because both my brother and I were rainbow babies—babies who were born after a miscarriage or a loss. My brother and I fulfilled our parents' dreams of having a healthy family.

So, when the doctor asked if either of our families had babies born with medical issues, I told him about my baby brother who had passed away. One day while joking with my mother-in-law about how she was able to maintain her sanity being the only woman with five men in her house—her ex-husband, who was Chris's dad; Chris; and his three older brothers—she told me that she, too, had suffered the loss of a child. It was something she and Chris's dad rarely spoke about. So much so that up until that time, Chris had only heard about that baby a couple of times in his life. His mom had told me the baby was a little girl, whom she had carried to full term. Sadly, the baby girl was born with the umbilical cord wrapped around her neck, and she had passed away in utero. I could see the joy mixed with sadness in my mother-in-law's eyes when she shared her story with me.

Chris and I each told the doctor about our siblings who had passed away, and although he took in the facts that we knew about both of our families, he homed in on the story about my baby brother. "Do you know what happened?" he asked me, while still taking measurements of our unborn son as I lay on the examination table.

"I don't know much other than what I told you," I said, concerned. What did my baby brother who died have to do with the baby I was carrying?

"Was that baby ever diagnosed with anything?" he continued.

"I...I don't know. I'm not sure," I told him. "All I know is my mom carried the baby and the doctors didn't know anything was wrong with him until after his due date. Then when my mom gave birth to him, he died a few hours later."

The doctor's eyebrows raised, and he asked another question: "Is your mother coming to your doctor's appointment later today?"

"No," I said, shaking my head from left to right.

"Why not?" the doctor asked sternly.

"I didn't know that I needed to bring her," I said, almost stammering.

"Well, she needs to be there," he told me in a fatherly tone.

"She does?" I asked, feeling like a child who had just been told her mom needed to go to school with her.

"Yes, she does," the doctor replied. "She may have some information that can help us."

"Okay," I said, as the doctor adjusted the sonogram table to the upright position.

"Danielle," the doctor said, looking into my eyes, "and Chris," he said, turning to look at my husband, "this is not your fault."

"Our baby's going to be okay, right?" I asked, as a tear fell from my eye. I was looking for some form of assurance that this entire nightmare was just that—a really bad dream that would end soon.

"This baby is not going to be okay. He is going to have significant mental and physical issues," the doctor said calmly in a very straightforward tone.

"Well, I believe our son is healthy," Chris said firmly, almost raising his voice to the doctor.

"Well, you can believe whatever you want to believe, but this baby is going to have some very difficult challenges. You are going to need a miracle in order for this baby to be healthy," the doctor said. He went on: "Now, I'm not saying that the two of you aren't deserving of a miracle. I am sure that that two of you are wonderful, wonderful people. And sometimes, bad things happen to really good people. What I want you to understand is that this is not your fault."

"Well, that's okay. We believe in miracles," I responded, allowing my faith to be on display. I figured if we ever needed to believe in a miracle, now was the time.

The doctor smiled at me and said, "Darlin', I want that for you too. But right now, we need to get a better understanding of what's going on with your baby. I want you to call your mom and tell her that she needs to be at the meeting with the two of you."

"Yes, sir," I said respectfully as more tears started to flow down my face.

"You're a great couple, and we're going to do our best to find out what's going on with your baby," the doctor said.

Chris and I both nodded, me with a slow, up-and-down movement and Chris with a quick and simple up-and-down of his head. The doctor patted me on the back, shook Chris's hand, and left the room.

Walking out to the car, I followed the doctor's orders and called my mom. I explained to her that the doctor said she needed to be at the appointment with us later that afternoon. I told her I'd told the doctor about her baby that passed away, and without hesitation she said she would be there. While I was calling my mom, Chris was calling his mom. Without sharing too much information, so as to not alarm her, he told her the doctor wanted to know about our family history regarding children born with medical abnormalities. During the six hours between our morning doctor's appointment and our team doctor appointments that afternoon, I tried to function as normally as possible, but I couldn't help but wonder what was going to happen later that day. Chris, on the other hand, was still confident. He kept repeating to himself and to me that "our boy is fine."

We began our afternoon of meetings with specialists and doctors from the fetal care center located within the local children's hospital. I was always amazed at the science and the technology that the fetal care center's doctors could use to change families' outcomes. To help correct medical issues, the doctors at the fetal care center could perform surgery on fetuses inside of their mother's womb. It was fascinating and intriguing to me how they were able to provide that level of care. Although the doctors' referral to the fetal care center denoted how serious our case was, I was confident that whatever our son's issues were, the doctors in the fetal care center would fix them. I went into our meetings thinking the doctors might tell us that they were initially wrong and the issues our son had weren't as serious as first believed.

My mom met us at the hospital for our afternoon of appointments. The first meeting we had was with a division of genetics social worker and a geneticist. They asked Chris, my mom, and me about our family history. The geneticist even had a family tree graph on a large, long sheet of paper that she filled out as we answered her questions. She wanted to know about siblings, grandparents, aunts, uncles, cousins—as much information as we had to give her, she wanted to know about it. Chris and I rattled off as much information as we knew, and on pieces that I either didn't know or couldn't recall, it was helpful that my mom was there to fill in the blanks. In the midst of them trying to figure out what our families' medical histories looked like, they also wanted to make sure Chris and I understood the severity of the prognosis our baby was facing. The social worker and geneticist asked us repeatedly, "Now that you have taken in all of this information, how do you feel? Are you okay?"

With strength in my spirit and sturdiness in my voice, I said, "Doctors practice medicine, but we know the Creator of it. And we talk to Him every single day." The geneticist nodded, but by the look on her face, either our situation was more serious than Chris and I understood, or he and I were just too naïve to really digest the information the doctors had presented. Nonetheless, the fact remained that we believed God would give us a miracle.

The geneticist went on to tell us that our baby's medical issues were very serious, and again, it was stated that some parents made the decision to terminate the pregnancy when faced with such circumstances. She did not try to persuade us one way or the other, but in doing her job as a medical professional and clearly stating the facts, she told us the cut-off date for an abortion in the state of Ohio was twenty-four weeks' gestation. Chris and I already had determined that no matter what, we were going to give our baby a chance to live. It was our personal belief that our baby was alive at the point of conception. And although we weren't going to judge anyone for what they chose to do based on their circumstances, for us, at twenty-two weeks and four days' gestation, we were not going to terminate our child.

The geneticist asked us if we had considered getting any genetic testing done on the baby or on ourselves to try to determine the reason for some of the medical issues. We told her no, and at that point, we weren't interested in doing so. In our minds, if we went through the genetic testing, it would be as though we were trying to find an issue with our baby. Chris and I were adamant that no matter what, we were going to love our child, and in our eyes, he was perfect—genetic condition or not, disability or not. The geneticist went on to explain that testing could help tell us what the rate of recurrence of these types of medical abnormalities would be in future children, but when asked if that would be something we were interested in, we told her no. We'd heard that genetic testing was expensive and we were already racking up several medical bills. And at that point, I was even more on board with Chris's one-child stance.

After about an hour of meeting with the geneticist, she led my mom, Chris, and me into a large room where we would have our team meeting. It was the most overwhelming experience I have ever had in my life. The three of us pulled chairs out from under the long rectangular table in the room, and I slowly turned my eyes upon all of the medical professionals who were there. At least seven doctors sat around the table, plus an administrative assistant; the geneticist who had spoken with us earlier in the day sat in the corner, and there were three more doctors sitting against the wall. At that moment, it occurred to me that this was more serious than Chris and I thought.

As the meeting began, there was a larger-than-life MRI image of our son on a black screen on one side of the room. The screen took up 75 percent of the wall; other than a movie theater screen or a big-screen television, it was the largest imaging screen I had ever seen in my life. And there, in the middle of the screen, was a milky white image of our little boy who was growing inside of me.

One of the doctors welcomed us into the room and started to talk about what he saw on the screen. When he paused, my mom, who had been mostly quiet outside of answering the questions the geneticist asked, spoke up. "Can everyone please introduce themselves to us?" she asked. Her question broke some of the heaviness that was in the air, and even the doctors seemed to relax a little at her proposition.

"Sure," one of them began. One by one, each person in the room introduced himself or herself. When I heard some of their titles and the divisions they represented, it confused me as to why they were there. There were cardiologists, neurologists, a neurosurgeon, high-risk maternal fetal medicine specialists, an otolaryngologist, the administrative assistant to the high-risk maternal fetal medicine doctor, residents who were studying to become specialists, and the three of us.

The doctors began explaining what each of them saw in respect to their individual disciplines. I appreciated that when they talked to us about our son, the referred to him as "Baby Christopher" instead of just calling him "the baby." Chris tried to get them to call the baby "Junior," and of the many who were there, one of them, much to Chris's liking, obliged. I'd decided that because my husband was so excited about his little "Junior," I would do my best to call him "Junior," too.

Collectively the doctors went from the crown of Baby Christopher's head all the way to his feet and explained to us what they saw. The prognosis was even worse than what we had initially been told. The first set of doctors who detected problems were limited in terms of what they could see and diagnose based on the sonogram pictures only. But with the MRI snapshots, this group of doctors was able to pinpoint every single issue and tell us what exactly we were up against. The ever-so-studious note taker in me pulled out the small blue notebook and pen that the geneticist had given me earlier in the day, and I began taking notes on everything the doctors were saying. I wrote as fast as I could, so as not to miss anything. My mom took notes as well, and Chris listened attentively as they spoke.

Some of the same issues that had been shared with us before were shared with us again. But this time, even more issues were presented to us. The doctors told us Junior probably had an abnormal chromosome disorder that would prove fatal. They told us his eyes were too far apart, his ears were low-set, and he had a slight cleft palate. They said he had fluid on his brain and would need a permanent shunt to drain the fluid. They told us the smooth parts of his brain were supposed to be bumpy, and the bumpy parts were supposed to be smooth. They told us his brain was missing a vermis, a critical part that is sometimes referred to as the central part where cognitive development and coordination of movement take place. Junior's ventricles were enlarged, and he was missing a portion of the back of his brain. Because of this, the doctors knew he had a Dandy Walker malformation. Because of the Dandy Walker malformation, the doctors told us our son would be severely physically and mentally disabled. They told us very straightforwardly that our son would probably never live away from us—even into his adult years. He probably never would do even simple things on his own, such as button a shirt or feed himself. They told us he had an abdominal wall cyst, as well as an omphalocele where part of his bowel was growing into his umbilical cord. That sounded horrific, but the doctors told us that with a small procedure, that could be fixed. In fact, the omphalocele was the least of our son's major issues. They told us that his wrists were clubbed and his feet were deformed. Based on what they saw, his pituitary and thyroid glands were extremely small. They told us his chin was too small and it appeared that his airway was extremely small, so they weren't sure if he'd be able to breathe on his own immediately after birth. And from the amnio fluid that was around the baby, it didn't appear he was taking in as much fluid as he should've been, which indicated to them that his airway was constricted. They knew all of these medical issues pointed toward some type of syndrome, but they weren't quite sure what that was.

In addition to this, because of the nature of all of his medical issues, I wouldn't even be able to hold Junior initially when he was born. The doctors would perform the C-section, show him to me, and then whisk him off to the NICU to possibly start some of the emergency procedures. Not being able to hold my baby after he was born was unfathomable to me. It was only natural for a mama to be able to hold her baby, and they were telling me this wouldn't happen.

During the meeting, Chris, my mom, and I asked a few questions the doctors told us were well thought out. I think they were even a bit impressed that Chris and I had already done some searching on our own about the medical conditions we had been told about. My mom brought up the fact that her son who passed away never gave off the right chemical signals to initiate labor and that was what alerted her and her doctors to the fact that something was wrong with him. My mom wanted to know if our baby would give off the signals that her baby had not. Chris and I asked questions about some of the specific issues the doctors had previously told us about. I asked what the difference was between a Dandy Walker malformation and Dandy Walker syndrome, since one of the doctors told us that the absence of our son's vermis could indicate he was on the Dandy Walker spectrum. Chris asked about our son's ability to understand and his ability to move around, given the doctor's diagnosis of the baby missing the coordination and cognitive reasoning parts of his brain. They told us that because of all of the fluid on his brain and his enlarged ventricles, I would have to have a C-section and Junior would be born at thirty-nine weeks.

Every so often, we would ask the doctors if there was any chance at all that our son would live a normal life, and unfortunately, the doctors would all get very quiet and then they would answer, "No." They told us they all had very serious concerns about our baby. Yet with all of these issues, they didn't have a definite medical diagnosis. Although the baby aligned with some symptoms of certain illnesses, his symptoms didn't align perfectly with any one specific illness, and that left the doctors a little confused. They didn't know what to call what our son had, but they knew what they saw from all of his test results. They flipped through numerous MRI slides to prove their points and told us what we were looking at and how it should've looked at that gestational age.

On the table, a box of tissues sat directly in front of me, but I was determined not to cry. I was this child's mama, and when they told me our baby was sick, it was my job and duty to be strong. The doctors could say what they wanted to, but I had an inner resolve that was made of steel, and it wasn't going to be tainted by tears—at least not at that moment on that day.

One of the doctors explained to us that our son's conditions were so severe that he would possibly be a candidate for a procedure known as the EXIT procedure, a specialized surgical delivery procedure used to deliver babies who had airway-compression issues. If an EXIT procedure was needed, an opening would be made on the midline of my anesthetized abdomen and uterus. After that, the baby would be partially delivered through the opening but remain attached by its umbilical cord to the placenta, while a pediatric otolaryngologist (head and neck surgeon) established an airway so the fetus could breathe. Once the EXIT procedure was finished, the umbilical cord would be clamped, then cut, and the baby would be delivered via C-section.

After all of these explanations, the doctors asked us a question I never expected to hear: "If the baby is born and he isn't breathing, what do you want us to do?" I sat numb for a second. Did they really think our baby would be born not breathing? Even with all of the medical problems they listed, I wasn't expecting for them to say Junior could be born not breathing. That never even crossed my mind. But as soon as it hit my mental processing center where I could actually think about what they said, my initial thought was to not let him suffer and to let him pass away. For goodness' sake, if he were born not breathing, I didn't want him suffering. But before my words could travel from my brain to my mouth, my husband spoke up. "You do everything you can do to save my boy," he said with a stern voice.

"Okay, we'll do what we can to save him," the doctors replied. As soon as that short exchange was over, I had never been so glad to have my husband speak for the both of us. I liked Chris's answer a lot better than the answer I was going to give, so I remained silent. I almost felt guilty. Chris was adamant about the doctors saving our son, and I was just about to let him pass away if he were born not breathing. Shame on me.

Almost ninety minutes after our meeting began, it ended with the doctors telling us that from that point on, I would need to be seen at the high-risk maternal-fetal medicine offices every Monday until the baby was due. Toward the end of my pregnancy, I would need to be seen twice a week—once on Monday and again on Thursday. At the Thursday appointments, the doctors would examine the baby and give him non-stress tests to see if he was responding as he should be. Making light of the fact that I would be going to the doctor every

Monday for the next seventeen weeks, I proudly announced that I was joining the "high-risk sisterhood." We and the doctors laughed at my joke, but we all knew how serious our circumstances were.

They asked us if we had any other questions before we left the meeting, and we quietly said no. As we were all walking out of the meeting room, Chris whispered to me, "Tonight is my bowling night, and the practice round starts at 6:30. It's already 6." He really wanted to get to the bowling alley on time, and I nodded back at him, knowing this bowling league was something he looked forward to and that he needed a stress reliever, tonight of all nights.

Chris always takes everything in stride. He was convinced that his boy would be fine, even after the doctors told us all they saw. Even though others may have thought his comment about bowling was callous, Chris saw himself as having a positive outlook about our situation. He had heard many stories about doctors who misdiagnosed children, and he believed that our situation would have the same outcome. In his mind, there was no reason to get worked up over nothing. He would stay optimistic, no matter what. One of the doctors had said he hoped our son would prove the doctors wrong. For Chris, if there were even a 1 percent chance that Junior could do so, then that was what Chris was going to believe.

+ + +

I had gone through twelve years of grade school, sitting in front of teachers every day as they taught me the basics of primary, middle, and high school education. I had persisted through four years of undergraduate college, where I had been a student of books and of life as I learned how to become an adult away from my parents. I had endured three and a half years of graduate school while studying almost every night of the week, taking tests, and working on major projects to earn my MBA. And yet, when I walked out of that meeting room that day, I felt like I had taken in more information than I ever had taken in before. In my mind, from that point forward, we had a whole seventeen weeks for God to work an awesome miracle.

As the geneticist walked us toward the door of the fetal care center, Chris spoke up: "I want us to get a second opinion." I looked at him, bewildered. The doctors had MRI proof of everything happening in our son's body. I thought getting a second opinion would mean that I'd have to go through another MRI, which meant more medical expenses.

The geneticist turned and asked Chris where he wanted to go to get a second opinion. He mentioned the name of a hospital that wasn't far from the children's hospital we were currently at, nor was it far from the main hospital where I was already being seen. In fact, those three hospitals were the hospitals involved in the collaborative effort that made up our city's fetal care center.

"Babe," I quietly said, "the doctors at that hospital also work at this hospital. They all share the same information. They're only going to tell us the same thing."

"Well, it doesn't matter. I still want to get a second opinion," he told me and the genetics doctor.

"Well, okay," the doctor said. "I'll get your files for you and have them transferred to the other hospital." Chris was satisfied with her answer and we left the fetal care center.

Walking through the halls of the medical center to get to our cars seemed like one of the longest walks of my life. Chris was walking fast because he was anxious about getting to bowling; my mom seemed slightly overwhelmed by all of the information we'd learned; and I was just numb. Up until that point, that was the worst day of my life. I'd figured that if Chris was going to enjoy his night at the bowling alley, then I was going to go where I would get some sort of peace and could enjoy my night too. I was heading to my church's midweek service.

In church, I sat near the back, next to one of my friends. I told her in the middle of service a little about what was going on, and she comforted me and told me she would pray for me. The pastor preached that night about God and His *kairos* timing, referring to the Greek word that means a moment in time when a significant event would take place. I truly believed that message was for us. We needed God to show up on our behalf in such a powerful way in our lives. For the first time since I had been pregnant, the baby moved more than I had ever felt him move. As the pastor preached, it felt like the baby was doing somersaults in my stomach. He bounced around as if he understood what the pastor was preaching about.

Toward the end of service, the pastor had an altar call, and he specifically asked for people who needed a God-given miracle to come up front. If I ever needed a God-given miracle, it was that day. My friend took me by the hand and walked with me to the front of the church. As the pastor and other care pastors started praying for me, I started weeping and could not stop. That night, I cried almost as hard as I'd cried on the day we found out we were having a little boy and that doctors had diagnosed him with multiple abnormalities. Before the service was over, the pastor's wife hugged me, and again, I sobbed uncontrollably as she held me tightly and whispered a powerful prayer and loving words into my ear. My inner resolve of steel had been broken, and I was emotionally spent.

CHAPTER TWELVE

The week after our initial fetal care center meeting, Chris and I went to the other hospital in town for his second opinion. After filling out paperwork and going through one sonogram, the head doctor of that medical center's fetal practice met with us. Though the doctors at our first team meeting were medically accurate in their findings, this doctor took some extra time with us and broke down the medical terminology. He made it easy to understand.

Since our team meeting, Chris had become very concerned about the doctors saying they couldn't find the vermis in our son's brain. He and I had spent hours on the Internet trying to learn more about the vermis, what it was and what it did, and if people didn't have a vermis, what their quality of life was. We found stories of people who didn't have vermises who lived normal lives. But we also found stories of people who were completely incapacitated due to not having a vermis. The spectrum was wide.

The second-opinion doctor drew us a diagram of what a healthy person's brain looked like and what our son's brain looked like. We could really begin to understand what some of the issues were that our son was facing. The doctor also shared an analogy with us that gave us a sense of hope. He told us that many times when people are born missing limbs, they are able to compensate for their movements with the limbs they do have, because that's all they've ever known. He gave us the example of a person born with only one arm. That person probably would figure out a way to go through life with his or her one arm, learning how to do the same things people with two arms do. Such people would never see themselves as being deficient. Still, he couldn't say something similar would be true for our son. He told us he didn't know if Junior would know the difference between Chris joking and being serious, or if he would just stare at Chris because his mental capacity would allow him only to realize that Chris was his father.

Chris asked that doctor more than one time and in more than one way if our son would be able to imagine. To Chris, that was everything. He knew that if our son could at least imagine, then he would have a sense of hope. Even if he were wheelchair-bound, Chris knew that if Junior could imagine that he was not, then one day he could actually start walking. If Junior could imagine, he would have a way of escape from the difficult picture of a life the doctors were painting for him. The doctor told Chris that he wasn't sure if our son would be able to imagine. But he did know that the type of home provided to our baby could make all the difference in the world. He and the initial doctor who had requested I bring my mom to our team meeting both said the same thing. They told us about how families could give birth to completely healthy children, give them horrible home lives, and the children then had horrible outcomes. They then also told us that, from their experiences, there were children unhealthy at birth who went home to loving families who cared for them and who never treated them differently because of their disabilities, and those children lived very full and amazing lives. The doctors drove that point home to us. They knew that our baby, no matter what the diagnosis, would come home to Chris and me. The doctors continued to tell us that no matter what happened with our son, they knew our son's life would be full because our son would be coming home with us. We were loving, sweet, dedicated parents when our child was still growing inside of my womb. All of those things would only grow once he was born.

We left that meeting feeling a little bit better about our situation. Because all the doctors we'd seen worked together, we figured we would return to the initial hospital where we started. We were getting good care, and we knew the doctors wanted to help us.

The highlight of going for the second opinion was that we got our first 3-D ultrasound pictures of Junior. When the sonogram tech pointed out his head, hands, and eyes, it was a beautiful picture. Our little boy had his hands clasped right in front of his face, and he looked like he was praying. Yep, even he was praying for his miracle, along with his mommy and daddy.

+ + +

The week after our second opinion, my job threw a baby shower for me and my coworker friend who I would exchange first-time pregnancy stories with. We both received books, clothes, and toys for our precious babies who were on their way. But every card, handwritten note, and gift that I received reminded me that our little boy's future was hanging in the balance. I had only shared the details of our doctors' appointments with my boss and a small handful of other people. I didn't want to alarm anyone or make anyone sad, especially since there were three of us pregnant in the department. To my knowledge, the other expecting moms hadn't received bad news about their babies, so there was no reason for me to share our story. Plus, up to that point, I had done a good job of keeping my personal life personal. My coworkers were excited for us, and we were excited too. Chris and I truly were standing on faith and the belief that our son would be born just fine. In our minds, at that point, I would be pregnant for fifteen more weeks, and a lot could happen between now and the day that this baby made his entrance into the world. That day at the shower, I shed a few tears over how wonderful my coworkers were, and I felt blessed that no matter what, our son was going to be born into a supportive community of family, friends, and his parents' coworkers.

One of my favorite gifts I received at the shower was a book titled *Guess How Much I Love You*. It's the story of a parent rabbit who assures the baby rabbit that no matter what, he will love the baby rabbit more than anything in the whole wide world. One of the last lines of the book is the parent rabbit telling the baby rabbit, "I love you to the moon and back." It instantly became one of my favorite books, and I decided that night that I would read *Guess How Much I Love You* to our little boy in utero at least every few days until he was born. That phrase explained my love for him perfectly. I loved him to the moon and back, and there was nothing or no one who would ever be able to change that.

Over the next few weeks, Chris and I shared our secret of what the doctors said with a few more people, but purposely not with too many. We continued to speak life into our situation, meaning that we chose to speak positive words instead of negative words and we chose to believe for the best instead of expecting the worst. We knew the outcome looked grim, but that didn't mean we had to give into it. We couldn't decide what happened to us, but we definitely got to choose how we responded to it. So for the sake of our mental health and for the sake of our baby not feeling any stress, we chose to be joyous no matter what.

One group of people we shared our story with consisted of seven couples whom we had grown close to over the last several years. We knew our close family members would be praying for us, and I knew my pastor and his wife would be praying for us, but I wanted some additional people praying for us too. One of my close friends had recommended I get seven couples we trusted to believe and pray for us and with us. The plan would be for them to take one day out of every week to pray for us between the beginning of May and when the baby was born. My desire was that the couples who prayed for us would not only cover us in prayer, but that their individual marital relationships would grow too. Praying for us was going to be beneficial for everyone. I promised to keep our "super seven," as I called them, aware of all the changes we experienced via weekly text messages. I felt like we needed an army of people on our side to help us win this battle, and slowly but surely, we were getting our soldiers in place.

From then on, we began our routine of going to the maternal-fetal medicine office every Monday. Every week, the doctors would tell us what they saw and we would tell them what we believed. They would continue to tell us that our son was very ill and we, especially Chris, would tell them that we believed our son was healthy. Initially at doctor appointments I would ask several questions about how the doctors thought our son would turn out once he was born, but most weeks the only answer they could give us was, "We'll wait and see what happens." It was a frustrating situation for us to be in, and I'm sure it was frustrating for the doctors too. Due to what the doctors saw on the sonograms, our doctors could definitely diagnose our son with certain illnesses, but there were others for which our son would meet some of the requirements of the diagnosis but not all of them, so the doctors couldn't make a conclusive finding. The only answers they had for us were, "We don't know; we'll wait and see," or they would give us bad news. We weren't particularly thrilled about any of those responses, so we decided to stop asking questions. We figured by doing so, we would protect our peace and still be able to enjoy our pregnancy.

CHAPTER THIRTEEN

There were several ways we made a conscious effort to enjoy our growing baby as much as any other couple would. Every Sunday, Chris would take pictures of me in the same place in our townhome from the front and the side so we could see the progression of my baby bump. I'd found a Noah's ark decorative room set where the giraffe, zebra, and lion wall decals were all smiling and looked like they were having fun, and I put those up on the baby's walls. Chris mocked my decorations because he said our child was going to grow up thinking he could touch wild animals based on the smiling creatures he would see every day.

So Chris decided that he, too, would buy decorations. He got mad at me when I told him he couldn't replace my happy animal decals with life-sized wild animals that had been hunting for prey on our son's walls. (He said that if our son was going to look at animals on the walls, they needed to be real animals. At least that way our son wouldn't go to the zoo thinking he could actually play with the animals.) Instead, Chris bought two very large wall decals on which our son's name was spelled out. When a person walked into our son's room and looked to the right or looked at his closet door, they would see the happy animals. If they looked to the left, above his crib, they would see CHRISTOPHER JONES, JR. spelled out in blue and

CHRISTOPHER spelled out again in brown letters. The border around the room displayed the alphabet and the numbers 1–10. Chris and I may have not been able to agree on a theme for the baby's room, but we could agree on our child being smart and learning his numbers, colors, and alphabet.

Our decorations clearly had a little bit of me and a little bit of Chris, but my favorite decal in our son's room was the Bible verse I'd picked out to go on his wall. I'd placed it right in the center of the animals so it would be prominent. It was Jeremiah 1:5: "Before I formed you in the womb I knew you, before you were born I set you apart." That verse spoke everything to me that I needed to know about our son. Before he was ever even born, God knew him. And before he was born, God had designated him for a great purpose. No matter what the doctors were saying or what the tests showed, the fact still remained: We believed our son had been chosen to do something amazing.

We knew the doctors were telling us our son would be born sick, but whether he was or not, at some point, we were planning to bring him home from the hospital. And since Chris and I both wanted to be prepared for whenever we bought our son home, we decided to have a baby shower. Whether or not he was born sick, our baby would still need clothes to wear, he would still need developmentally appropriate toys to play with and learn from, and he would still need diapers and wipes and many of the other things people purchase for baby showers.

While registering items for the baby shower, Chris and I couldn't have been more different. While I added things like nail-clipper kits and bath gel to the registry, Chris complained, saying he had already bought everything the baby needed. His idea of "everything the baby needed" included all of the bigger items he had purchased earlier plus four bibs, two each that said "I love Daddy" and "My Daddy Is Better Than Yours." Chris even asked me why I was putting several sheet sets on the registry when the baby would need only one sheet to sleep on. As he complained, I shook my head, laughed, and kept using my registry gun to add items. Chris was going to be a funny daddy!

I'd heard varying accounts from women about the attention they received when they were pregnant. Some of them loathed it, while others loved it. I was on the latter end of that spectrum. I absolutely loved being pregnant and the attention I received because of the life I had growing inside of me. I didn't mind answering generic pregnancy questions, like if the baby was keeping me up at night or how many weeks pregnant I was. I got special perks like people allowing me to skip ahead in line while I waited to use a public restroom. People bought me free treats and food. I got to sneak food into theaters without getting in trouble with security, and I had even asked my employer to create special parking spaces so all of the pregnant women in my building wouldn't have to walk far to get to our cars.

So, on the day of our baby shower—June 6, 2015—I made sure to look as pretty as I possibly could. I wore a long turquoise dress and had been pampered at the salon early that morning. I'd also purchased new jewelry that matched my dress. My mom, aunts, and best friend worked hard to decorate our baby shower room beautifully. In keeping with my Noah's ark theme, we had a cute cake with the ark, plus happy animal cups, plates, and table decorations. Chris smirked at the decorations when he arrived, but he also told me he wanted me to be happy. Besides, he'd already won the battle of not having me put happy animals *all* over our son's room!

Chris and I decided to have a co-ed shower because we had male and female friends who were all cheering for our little family. We didn't want to exclude anyone from sharing our joy. I know baby showers aren't usually the biggest deal in the world, but our baby shower was everything to me. Second behind our wedding, it was the largest gathering we had where so many of our friends and family members came out to celebrate us. I was thrilled that sixty people shared our joy that day. We played games, ate, and opened gifts. To see our loved ones "ooh and ahhh" with us felt amazing. Reminiscent of my work baby shower, it truly felt like showers of love were coming down on us. Never to step outside of his "get it done" character, as soon as the shower was over, Chris and our families transported our gifts to our home. Then he was immediately ready to go to the store and use the gift cards we'd been given to purchase the last few items we still needed. By the end of that night, we had every material item we wanted to have before we welcomed our son into the world. All we needed was for him to be born and to be born healthy.

In addition to taking weekly progress pictures and having a baby shower, we also took the recommended first-time parenting classes offered at the hospital. We learned all about diapering babies, car seats, baby CPR, what to pack in a hospital bag, and what the birthing experience would be like. Chris even took a first-time fatherhood class. In every class, Chris and I sat in the front row and we asked more questions than our classmates. We wanted to know what we were doing. This would be our first time at this rodeo, and we wanted to make sure we got it right. At the end of one class, some of our classmates told us they were so happy to have us with them. We made people laugh and the instructors got a kick out of Chris's hand movements and interpretations of what the instructors were teaching. We were confident we were going to be good parents.

In the midst of us trying to figure out everything with the pregnancy, we knew that Chris's job contract would soon be ending and he would need to find a new job. In mid-June he was able to find a contract position at another large company. We couldn't have been more grateful for the support that his current team had given him. They showed that they cared about what the doctors were saying regarding our son's health, and Chris genuinely liked his work team. For the first time in a long time, Chris enjoyed the work he was doing and felt confident about it. He wasn't making a ton of money at the job, but he was happy and liked being there. To us, that was all that mattered. He came home happy every day. And for the four months that he was there, we were stable in our finances, which was great.

+ + +

In the weeks after the baby shower, Chris and I had another team meeting with the doctors in the fetal care center. This time around, although the outlook was still grave, the meeting didn't have the same heavy, depressing feeling that loomed over the first team meeting. The doctors realized that over the course of the previous two months, Junior had been taking in and swallowing some of the amniotic fluid that surrounded him, like he was supposed to. This showed that his airway was more open than initially thought, which meant we wouldn't have to go through an EXIT procedure. Instead, I'd be able to have a regular C-section.

I know a lot of women fought to have natural births, but not me. I was completely fine with the doctors performing surgery to remove my baby. I joked with the doctors that we got our son into my belly, but they would have to figure out a way to get him out. I had heard about the pain women experience going through natural births, and I didn't want to feel that pain. Plus, at that point, it was physically impossible for me to have a natural birth because of our son's head size. When I was only thirty-three weeks pregnant, his head size was measuring as though he were a forty-six-week-old baby. Because of this, the doctors had determined that they would need to deliver the baby at thirty-eight weeks, not at thirty-nine as they'd initially said. They wanted me to stay pregnant with the baby as long as possible, and we knew that was best also. Unfortunately, I still wouldn't be able to hold the baby when he was first born; I would only be able to see him to meet him. That made me really sad, and I would talk to Chris about it and he would console me. If that was what was best for the baby, then I would have to obey the doctor's orders.

From the end of June until the end of the pregnancy, I had to go to the doctor twice a week. Once on Monday for my high-risk maternal, fetal medicine appointment and once on Thursday so the baby could go through a non-stress test. The non-stress tests were measuring the baby's activity level and heart rate and my contractions. Chris and I had gotten used to me going to the Monday appointments. We would talk to the doctors and get sonogram pictures of the baby. We became enamored with the 3-D sonogram pictures, and we would ask for them every time we had an appointment.

During the first Thursday appointment, the baby didn't pass the initial non-stress test, meaning he didn't move around enough and his heart rate wasn't measuring the way it should have. So the technician who performed the test referred me for a backup non-stress test, which consisted of me having to get a sonogram to see how much the baby was performing spontaneous movements and if he was breathing within a certain amount of time. Thankfully, Junior did well on his "make-up" test and we got to leave the hospital. But during the following Thursday appointments, he didn't pass the initial non-stress tests, nor did he pass the make-up tests. And when he didn't pass the make-up tests, that meant I had to go to the labor and delivery department of the hospital. When a baby didn't pass the non-stress test, it gave the doctor cause for concern. It could indicate that the baby wasn't doing well in the womb, and the doctor could decide to induce labor.

At my Monday appointment after our first Thursday non-stress test appointment, the doctor broke the news that they would deliver the baby at thirty-seven weeks instead of thirty-eight. The baby's head was big, and with him failing the non-stress test, they weren't going to allow me to carry him any longer.

Because Chris had just started a new job, he was in training the day the doctor gave me our new due date. I called to tell him that, but I also wanted the doctor to give Chris some important medical advice. Chris was determined to have a vasectomy after our first child was born. When he shared this news with me, it caused me a lot of distress. Even though we were hoping for the best with this child, we didn't know how the circumstance was going to turn out. If he got a vasectomy, we wouldn't be able to have any more children. And while at times I loved my husband's decisive nature, there were times when the impulses of that nature were overwhelming to me. The doctor explained to him why he shouldn't have the permanent medical procedure done, but Chris wasn't taking in what he was saying. In fact, he already had called to schedule the vasectomy for mid-August.

That day and the following day, we argued via text and had some very heated discussions in person about his decision. I couldn't believe he would be making a decision like that, especially right now. As if we hadn't had enough to worry about already, he was only adding to the stress, and at that point, there was nothing anyone could say to change his mind.

July came, and we knew that before the end of the month, we'd have a baby in our arms. As another way to prep for the baby, we purchased a larger vehicle to accommodate our needs. We had packed our labor and delivery bag and had put it in our new vehicle. We had gotten our car seats safely secured from a certified car seat technician, and we were ready to go.

Although Chris wouldn't go with me because he didn't think we'd need to see it, I made an appointment to tour the children's hospital's NICU. I was still holding out hope that the baby would be born healthy, but just in case the doctors were right and he was in the NICU for several weeks, I wanted to see where he'd be going. Having worked at the same hospital where the doctors were saying our son would be a patient was a little scary, yet comforting at the same time. For years I had been able to tell stories about the awesome care our doctors, nurses, and staff had provided to families at the hospital, and because of this situation, I was about to have my own patient family story. As I walked through the halls of the NICU, a few things stuck out to me. I noticed that some of the beds and rooms had cameras so parents could watch their babies remotely twenty-four hours a day, seven days a week if they wanted to. The other thing I noticed was that there were different arrangements for the NICU patients' beds. Some of them were in large, open spaces called pods. And some of the beds were in individual rooms. The clinical director said that the amount of necessary care and the individual situation determined if a patient was in a private room. I didn't quite understand what that meant at the time, but I had decided that if we were going to be in the NICU, I definitely wanted to be in a private room.

One other thing we did to prep for the baby's arrival was to choose a pediatrician. Chris and I wanted to meet her before Junior was born, and I was so glad we did. She answered every question we had and she gave us additional medical education. Initially, we were overwhelmed by the idea of our baby needing to have a brain shunt put into his skull to drain the fluid off his brain. After she explained to us the dangers of not having that procedure done, we felt ten times better about doing it. She also explained to us how easily doctors could fix our son's omphalocele. It was probably the least of the issues our son was facing.

And thankfully, the pediatrician also was able to talk Chris out of getting a vasectomy. She spoke to him from the experience of a doctor who had seen families make a variety of decisions when it came to family planning. And she was able to help him understand that right after we had our baby might not be the best time for him to make such a permanent decision.

+ + +

Chris and I went to my parents' house for their annual Fourth of July celebration with family and friends. We laughed, talked, ate, danced, and ended the night by watching a fireworks show my dad put on. The Fourth of July would be one of the last times I'd be around our family and friends before the baby was born, and I enjoyed every minute of it. Our lives were getting ready to change in a big way, and I was grateful that we had so many people to spend our time with.

I decided it would be fun to write little notes to our son leading up to the day he was born and thereafter.

July 17, 2015, 5:48 p.m.
Ten days and waiting!!!
Dear Little Boy,

Your daddy and I are so excited to meet you. I can't believe that you will be here in ten short days. Wow! Your due date wasn't supposed to be until August 16, which technically means you are being born a few weeks early. As of right now, your head size is measuring like you are a forty-six-week-old baby even though you are really only about thirty-six weeks. You weigh 6.5 lbs. and you move around a lot in Mommy. In fact, you usually start moving at about 7 or 8 a.m.; then you stop around 8:30 a.m. Then you start moving again when Mommy eats lunch, then you move again when you and Mommy drive home together from work around 5 or 5:30 p.m., then you move around again at about 10 or 11 p.m. Then you move around again around 2 or 3 a.m.! Mommy loves feeling you move, roll, kick, and squirm inside of her! Well, as I close, I want you to know that you are loved so much! Your mommy, daddy, grandparents, uncles, big cousins, aunties, great-grandparents, and so many more people are looking forward to meeting you and kissing you and hugging you. It is amazing that God chose your daddy and me to be your parents. You are already a fighter, and you continue to prove the doctors wrong. We love you!

Saturday, July 18, 2015, 3:26 p.m.
Dear Little Boy (aka Junior),

Your Daddy and I are excited that we will get to meet you in nine short days! Today Mommy and Daddy are spending time with friends who are all excited about your pending arrival. Today it is very hot outside! I can't wait to see if you like the summer, winter, spring, or fall better. Today, as usual, you moved around when Mommy ate lunch, which is a very good thing. This morning, Mommy looked up information about how long it would take for you to recover from omphalocele and brain shunt surgery. Mommy and Daddy don't want you to have to have surgery, but we are okay if God decides to use the doctors and surgeons and surgery to heal your little body. We really just want you to come home happy. So we are going to continue to believe that God is going to continue to heal you on the inside of Mommy. He's already done so many miracles in your life, and we believe He's going to do many, many, many more!

Love you forever and always,

Mommy and Daddy

Sunday, July 19, 2015, 11:31 p.m.

Eight days and counting!

Dear Little Boy,

We are continuing to do the last-minute things we need to do as we await your arrival. Today Mommy bought some more stuff for you. Tomorrow morning we have a doctor's appointment where we'll get to see you on the sonogram screen. We like seeing you move around on there. You moved around today but not as much as Mommy is used to. I think it's getting kind of tight in that little space for you. Know that we are thinking of you, praying for you, and speaking life over you!

Love always,

Mommy and Daddy

Monday, July 20, 2015, 11 p.m.

Only seven days to go!

Dear Little Boy,

So I know you are probably going to get tired of me calling you, "Hey, Little Boy," but that's what I've called you since we found out you were a little boy! Before that, I called you "Baby Bump!" Your daddy calls you "My Boy" and "Junior." Your real name is Christopher (it means Bearer of Christ) Louis (it means Warrior and/or King) Jones (it means favor and grace of God) Jr. You are named after your daddy. The cool thing is that your middle name is the same as Mommy's maiden name—only her name was spelled "Lewis." Today's doctor appointment went well. But they told us if you slow down on your movement or if Mommy has six contractions in one hour, the doctors are going to deliver you. That means you may be here before next Monday. No matter what, Daddy and I are excited to meet you and are looking forward to holding you, hugging you, and kissing you.

Love always,
Mommy and Daddy

CHAPTER FOURTEEN

As I sat in the hospital bed with machines and monitors hooked up to me, the doctor asked me, "Do you know why we're delivering your baby today?"

"Because he keeps failing all of the non-stress tests," I answered matter-of-factly and to the best of my ability.

"We're delivering your baby today because we don't want you to have a stillborn baby," he responded.

"Oh," I said as I sat back against the bed, not having expected his response. We were having a baby, and he was coming fast.

+ + +

The days leading up to Tuesday, July 21, had been different than the other days during my pregnancy. That previous Saturday, I had been tired and almost lethargic. I noticed I was starting to have slight contractions, and when I called the emergency nurse's line, she told me to start counting them and if I were having more than six in an hour, to come into the hospital. I decided to spend the day with a good girlfriend, and she persuaded me to take it easy even though I wanted to run a few errands in preparations for the baby. That Sunday, I went to church as usual, but I noticed Junior wasn't moving around as much as he usually did. He usually bounced all around when the praise and worship team was singing and when the pastor's voice boomed through the loud speakers in the sanctuary. And by that time Junior had developed a routine: He would move and twirl around inside of me at about 8 a.m., during the lunch hour, at around 3 p.m., at around 5 p.m., and then around 11 p.m. But on that Sunday he hardly moved at all. The doctors told me the importance of making sure I was counting how many times he moved around, and if I noticed that he wasn't moving around as much, I would need to alert them. A healthy baby would move at least ten times within two hours. But Junior usually moved ten times in less than a minute.

So when he was hardly moving that Sunday, I got a little scared. I knew that sometimes babies didn't move as much because the space around them was getting smaller as they grew bigger in their mother's uterus. But this time, it seemed a little weird that he wasn't moving as often. There was only one other time during the pregnancy when he wasn't moving much, and Chris got down on his knees and cupped my stomach between his hands and started coaching our son to move. And Junior responded to Chris's voice. But on this particular Sunday, nothing seemed to get him going. Even my high-pitched squeal of "Little Boyyyyyy, it's your mama" didn't work. I ran errands and he still wasn't doing much. So when I got home, I sat in bed and started my kick-counting app on my phone. Junior didn't move ten times, and it had been almost an hour.

The next day, I had a regularly scheduled doctor's appointment and when I told the doctor about the baby not moving around as much, he was very concerned. He told me that if I continued to notice any changes with our son's movement or with how I was feeling, I needed to come into the hospital immediately and the doctors probably would have me deliver the baby. That afternoon at work, while walking down the hallway, I suddenly felt as though I were on a roller coaster. It seemed the baby had dropped within me. His due date was right around the corner, and because of what I'd just felt, he was coming soon.

+ + +

In the midst of us preparing for our baby's arrival, Chris's contract at his new job ended only ten business days after it started. According to his boss, he was on his cell phone too much. I felt a little guilty about that, because during the days while he was at his new job, he and I would text about any news we'd receive from the doctors regarding the baby. And over those ten days, we had a lot that we had to communicate about. From finding out that the baby would be born earlier than expected, to the high-risk maternal, fetal medicine doctor and me trying to convince him to not get a vasectomy, to us trying to figure out what our course of action would be over the next few weeks as the baby came, Chris was on his phone more than usual. He had explained to his boss that his wife was a high-risk pregnancy patient and that we had to communicate frequently throughout the day, but nonetheless he lost his job.

Chris and I, seeing a positive side to everything, viewed this time of him losing his job as somewhat of a blessing. Losing his job would mean a decrease in our household income (again), but it would also mean that he would definitely be there for our child's birth. And that was priceless. Ironically, the day after he lost his job, another company he had been interviewing with called and made him a job offer. They wanted him to start in two weeks.

On the morning of July 21, I went into work and just didn't feel normal. I was already moving much more slowly than I was used to because I'd gained fifty pounds over the course of the pregnancy.

My left foot was extremely swollen and the doctors had prescribed me compression tights to wear. Because of the swelling, I had been confined to wearing what I called "Jesus sandals" for the last several weeks. They were clunky, men's open-toe hiking sandals, but they were the only shoes I could find that were big enough to actually fit my growing foot. And although I was enjoying being pregnant, my limited mobility and the increased nausea due to the extra fluid around the baby were beginning to take a toll on me. On that day, the baby still wasn't moving around much, and the doctor's warning about me coming into the hospital if I'd noticed any changes stuck with me.

Around noon I called my husband and told him I was concerned. "What do you think we should do?" I asked him.

"What do *you* think we should do?" he asked me in response. "You're the mom. They're going to listen to you more than anyone else."

"I think we should go to the hospital. I'd rather be safe than sorry," I responded. The doctors had already planned my C-section to take place the following Monday, July 27. But I figured that if we went to one more Thursday appointment and the baby didn't pass the non-stress test, they probably would decide to give me a C-section then.

So I figured that on Tuesday we'd go to the hospital around 12:30 p.m. for observation and they'd send me home. But I was wrong. Here we were at 2:30 p.m., and the doctor was telling me they didn't want us to have a stillborn child so we were going to have the baby in about two hours. At that moment, I remembered them saying something about him being born not breathing, but I hadn't equated that in my mind to having a stillborn baby. At the time, Chris wasn't in the hospital room and the doctor asked me the same question they asked us in our initial team meeting, when Chris so adamantly told them our answer. "If the baby is born not breathing, what do you want us to do?"

I locked my eyes with his and firmly said, "You do everything you can do to save him." The doctor nodded and said okay, and our birthing story began.

The doctor then looked at me and told me that because of the type of C-section I needed, I shouldn't get pregnant again for at least twelve to eighteen months. I sat stunned by the directive. Twelve to eighteen months seemed like an eternity from that moment, and I didn't understand why I needed to wait so long. I had heard of other women having babies who got pregnant within months after giving birth, so why did I have to wait so long? If our baby was indeed born with multiple issues or if he passed away shortly after his birth, I didn't want to wait twelve to eighteen months to get pregnant. But the doctor delivered some news to me that I hadn't heard before or even considered.

"Mrs. Jones, most women get a bikini-cut C-section," the doctor started. I knew that a bikini-cut C-section was a cut along a woman's bikini line. "But because of your baby's head size, we need to give you a bikini cut and a classical-cut C-section, which means you will be cut twice. You will have a line going up and down your uterus as well as a line across your bikini line." In my mind, I equated his explanation to me having a "T" on my uterus. "You will need to wait twelve to eighteen months before you have another baby so your uterus doesn't rupture."

That was like a punch to my gut, but it drove home the point of why I definitely didn't want to get pregnant until the doctor said I could. God, I wanted Junior to be born healthy, because I didn't know what I would do for twelve to eighteen months waiting to get pregnant again if he were not.

As I lay flat on the hospital gurney, with a team of nurses, doctors, an anesthesiologist, and Chris walking alongside of me, I was excited to meet this little boy who had caused so much commotion in our lives. They had both of us hooked up to monitors, and when it was time for us to leave the observation room, it was as if he knew his eviction notice from my stomach was being served and acted upon. His heart rate sped up, and as only I could, I tried to calm him. "It's okay, Little Boy, we're excited to meet you," I repeatedly told him.

Chris chimed in: "It's okay, Junior. Daddy's here. We're looking forward to meeting you."

As they rolled me down the hallway to the operating room where the C-section would be performed, I asked about a room that we passed where I saw medical equipment set out on a table. My inquisitive nature prompted me to ask about what I saw. "What is that room for?"

"Oh, that's where babies go if they need a little help after they're born," replied a nurse. That was a sufficient answer for me as I tried to relax.

Always one to reflect on Bible verses when times were hard in my life, I tried to recall any of them that would help comfort my and my baby's nerves as we were preparing to bring Junior into the world. But no matter how hard I tried, the only Scripture that would come to mind was Psalms 23. It wasn't one of the Scriptures I reflected on often, but on this day, at this time, it was the only one that my mind would rehearse over and over again. Even as I tried to force my brain to focus on something else, that Scripture still prevailed in the forefront of my mind. It was as if I had no choice but to etch that on my heart and silently speak it. Chris had been saying it aloud over the last few weeks, and now, I too, was forced to say it.

> The Lord is my shepherd, I shall not want. He makes me lie down in green pastures, He leadeth me beside still waters, He refreshes my soul. He guides me down the path of righteousness. For His name's sake. Yea, though I walk through the valley of the shadow of death, I will fear no evil, for thou are with me. Thy rod and thy staff comfort me. You prepare a table before me in the presence of my enemies. You anoint my head with oil and my cup overflows. Surely your goodness and mercy will follow me all the days of my life, and I will dwell in the house of the Lord forever.

I had mainly heard the 23rd Psalm talked about at funerals and sad occasions, so I didn't want to repeat it here. Not now. But no matter how hard I tired, it was the only thing that would come to me.

CHAPTER FIFTEEN

Tuesday, July 21, at 4:41 p.m., our son, Christopher Louis Jones Jr., was born. He was not breathing, and he was blue. The doctor held him up for Chris and me to see him and immediately carried him out of the room.

Chris and I both, almost in unison, asked, "Did he cry?" Even with the doctors telling us about all of the baby's issues, we still held onto the hope that he would cry when he was born. But we didn't hear anything as the doctor held him up. We then both asked, "Why is he blue? Is he okay?"

The nurse who was holding my hand at the top of the gurney, near my head, spoke up. "He's okay; he just needs a little help. The doctors are helping him and you're doing great," she said in a calm, motherly tone.

Chris, who had been doing a great job coaching me along the way, agreed with her. "Yeah, babe. You're doing great."

But I knew what the nurse's response really meant. Our baby was being taken to the room we had passed on the way into the operating room. Our baby was one of the ones who needed help in order to live.

Chris: On that day, I was scared but excited. I was anxious to meet my boy. My plan was to be the best father in the world, not through spoiling but love. I had plans to get my son in trouble with my wife.

It was going to be fun. At this time, my wife was in the delivery bed and I was sitting in a chair beside her. The doctor on staff came into the room and asked my wife, "Do you know why we are taking the baby?" He told her the reason for delivering the baby now was to avoid a stillbirth. I was calm and excited.

My wife received an epidural. I sat by her head, gaining excitement. I looked at my wife and told her she was doing a good job. I listened intently for my boy to cry but heard no sound. One of the doctors told us he had been born, but still I heard no sound. A doctor had him in her arms and showed him to us as she was walking out of the room. Literally, he was blue like a Smurf. We were told he wasn't breathing and they had to transport him to another room. I got up to follow him only to be halted and told that they would notify me when I could see him. I remember sitting back down and exclaiming to my wife that I needed to see him. I wanted to pray over him and declare his health.

Finally, after what seemed like forever, the nurse came to get me and told me I could see him. I walked into the area where he was being kept and saw a tube in his mouth and a nurse sitting by his side with what seemed to be a hand pump. He turned from a blue complexion to a light reddish brown color. When I walked into the room, I said, "That's my boy!" And he immediately jumped. He knew his daddy was talking to him. I was so happy because his reaction let me know that he knew me. He knew I was his father.

The nurse was pumping oxygen into my boy. She told me he was getting prepped to be transported to the children's hospital. I figured this would be a good time to visit my wife, who had been taken to a recovery area. Half of my wife's body was numb, but she was alert. She told me she was doing okay from the cuts and the epidural. She inquired about our son, and I told her that he was no longer blue. I also told her there was a nurse pumping air into his body. My hope was that she could see him.

I sat with her for a while before our son was transported to the children's hospital. As a father and a husband, I really didn't know who to spend my time with. The two most important people in my life were going to be in two separate hospitals. My wife encouraged me to go to the children's hospital to visit our son as soon as he had been transported there.

Danielle: After they wheeled me into a recovery area, I lay there with Chris by my side. We'd called my parents to tell them about the baby being born, and within an hour of his birth, they both arrived to the hospital. Shortly after his birth, the doctors brought Junior into the recovery area so I could see him. He was so tiny, yet so big at the same time. I couldn't believe that this little live person had come out of me. Because he was in an incubator infant bed, I could only hold his hand through a tiny hole. He was jittering and shaking, which alarmed me, but as I held his hand, I repeated, "It's okay. Mama's here, baby. Mama's here."

I studied our baby as he lay there, helpless. He had the oversized head that we saw on the sonogram screen, and his chin was almost nonexistent. But he gripped my finger, which let me know he was alive and he was a little fighter.

Two EMTs stood by my bed and told us Junior would need to be transported immediately via ambulance to the children's hospital, which was only a few blocks away. I told Chris to go with Junior so he wouldn't be alone without either of his parents. My parents said they would sit with me until after we got everything situated for the night and until Chris could return to the main hospital to spend the night with me.

Chris: When I got to the children's hospital, it was the longest walk of my life going to my son's room in the NICU. Finally, after registering, I reached my son's room. I was devastated and I jumped when I walked into his room. I was startled to see my son connected to a life-support machine. The doctor on call explained to me that my son was not able to support his own life and thus he needed a ventilator to breathe for him.

Danielle: That night, Chris came back to the main hospital around midnight, clearly flustered and frustrated. My parents and I tried to calm him and ask him what was wrong, but he was visibly upset. I had never seen him so shaken before. Chris's playful and jovial nature was completely gone. He told us the baby wasn't well and that he was hooked up to a ton of machines and that at that point, no one could give him any additional answers. His eyes were red. His tie and business shirt he'd had on from earlier that day were now loose.

He then started rambling in a loud voice, "The baby isn't doing good. He's in critical condition, and I don't understand!" My parents and I all looked at him with sad eyes, but we let him finish getting his frustrations out.

After Chris calmed down a bit, my parents made sure we were situated in the hospital room for the night, gave us hugs and kisses, and told us they would check on us the next day.

We fell asleep, Chris on the pull-out bed in the room and me in the hospital bed, exhausted, scared, and with our nerves wrecked from the events of that day.

CHAPTER SIXTEEN

Day 1:

The morning after our son was born, Chris and I both woke up around 7:30 a.m. Though we were still groggy and trying to make sense of the evening before, Chris remembered that he had an MS infusion appointment scheduled for 8:30 that morning. Thankfully, his appointment was at the same hospital where I had delivered, only in a different part. Never one to be late to any type of appointment, he kissed me on my forehead and told me he needed to get to his treatment. But only thirty minutes after leaving my room, he returned, upset and looking helpless. "They said I can't get my treatment today." He had always been able to get his treatment, and to our knowledge, there was no reason why things should have been different that day. "They told me I'm not authorized," he said, shrugging his shoulders angrily.

My company's insurance provider switched on July 1 and all of our medical history hadn't yet been uploaded into the new insurance provider's system. I was a patient at the hospital after having given birth, our son was a NICU patient at a different hospital, and my husband needed to receive medical care, too, but could not because of an authorization clause in our insurance. It seemed as though we were in the middle of a medical mess. All three of us had serious medical issues to tend to, and we needed help in the biggest way possible.

Since Chris couldn't get his infusion, he decided he would go home to get cleaned up and bring a few items back to the hospital for me and for Junior. He kept repeating that he needed to get to his boy to see him. My only request of him when he went home was to bring back the book *Guess How Much I Love You* so I could read it to Junior as soon as I was able to go see him.

The doctors and nurses told me that if I was feeling well, I would be able to go and visit the baby at the hospital on a four-hour-a-day pass. That sounded great to me. I couldn't wait to be near my baby and hopefully, at some point soon, hold him. I would do everything I needed to do to get well enough to go see him.

Later that morning, every so often, I'd hear a chime go off in the hallway. After hearing the chime a few times, I asked one of the nurses what the chime meant. She shared with me that every time someone had a baby, the chime would go off. From then on, when the chime went off, I was happy for the parents who were having a baby, but I was also praying they weren't going through heartache like ours.

Chris: When I got to the hospital on the first full day of him being there, I walked into our son's room and went to gently rub his chest and tell him I loved him. I wasn't sure if he would live long, but my decision was that he would experience love while he was here on earth. Suddenly, an occupational therapist walked into the room and asked me, "Would you like me to show you how to love your child?" Eager to see what she could show me, I told her yes.

She walked me over to his right foot and gently cupped his heel. She told me his heel was the place where doctors wanted to draw blood. She told me Junior needed to feel a touch in the hurt place, which in this case was his foot, to know that every touch was not intended to cause pain. That meant the world to me. She further explained that any chance of surviving increases drastically when a child experiences the love of his parents. I was anxious for his mom to come love on him. I had learned through pre-birth classes that women were literally built to be mothers. The problem was that my wife, too, was in the hospital attempting to heal from her wounds.

It was a ray of hope when my wife called and told me she could come visit the baby that day, because I believe women have healing power within them. I waited until noon and drove to pick her up from the main hospital. She was in a wheelchair, and she would have to be in one when I took her to go see Junior. I learned that I needed to relieve as much labor off her body as possible. I felt good being able to finally bring her to Junior. I showed her how to love Junior as I was taught. My desire was for her to pick him up and hold him against her bosom, but Junior was fully connected with tubes and wires so she couldn't lift him.

Throughout the day, multiple doctors visited the room. I call them "Ologists" because I couldn't remember all of their titles, but I knew all of their titles ended with "-ologist." They asked me, "What do you desire for your son?" The only thing I ever told them was I didn't want him to suffer.

Junior had a tube coming out of his throat, he was pricked everywhere, and he would grimace and open his mouth as if he were trying to scream or cry. It was painful for me to watch my son in pain. He was given medicine to ease the pain, but I just wanted his suffering to cease. In the back of my mind, I knew that all of that pain could eventually have death attached to it, and I spent time emotionally preparing for it.

That night I wanted to be near my boy, so I spent the night in his hospital room. I stood over my son and told him I needed him in my life. I then burst into uncontrollable tears. I was fortunate that no one walked in; it allowed me to grieve. I then lay down on the couch and went to sleep.

Danielle: I was finally able to go see the baby, and as soon as I arrived, it hit me that this was not a good situation. I remember my NICU tour and the clinical director telling me that depending on how much care a patient needed helped determine what type of room he was placed in. When I realized that Junior was in a private room instead of an open pod with several other babies, I knew he was one of the sickest babies on the NICU floor. Initially I wanted to be in a room where it was just our little family, but now I realized that the babies in the pods probably weren't as ill and that would've meant a better outcome for us.

Junior was in the middle of an incubator bed, but there were intimidating machines and equipment all around him. A huge warming lamp was above him. Chris and I started referring to it as the rotisserie light, because underneath it, Junior looked like a plump little hen baking.

The nurses and doctors surrounded his bed, and it hurt me that they had been able to see my baby and spend time with him—the one I had carried inside of me for almost nine months—before I'd had a chance to.

It was nice being able to spend time with him, but every few minutes, there were doctors and nurses coming in to see him, writing down information, assessing him. I didn't feel like we had any time to spend together as a family. One of the best parts of the day was when Chris was excited to show me what he had learned from one of the occupational therapists regarding how to touch our son so he would feel loved by us. But other than that, I was overwhelmed by everything that was taking place in that hospital room.

That day, the doctors gave me a little stuffed animal called a snoodle. They told me to sleep with and wear it so my scent would rub off onto it. When I brought it back to the hospital the next day, the nurses would place it in our son's isolette bed so he could smell me and be comforted. They said they would place a snoodle near Junior, too, so his scent could rub off on it, and then I could have it while I was away from him.

When I got back to my hospital room that night, my milk started to come in. It was as if I needed to see and smell my baby in order for my milk to finally start. When it came in, I felt like a normal mom. I might not have been able to hold my baby yet, but I could finally start doing my part of producing food for him. I smiled that night. Maybe our lives weren't going to be as bad as it seemed after all.

Day 2:

Danielle: On Day 2, my aunt and my grandmother picked me up from the hospital to go see the baby. We had gotten help from our family members to transport me back and forth from the children's hospital to the main hospital so Chris could always stay with Junior. However, we had chosen not to share much information with them about the baby's medical condition because we didn't want to alarm them. This would be my grandmother's first great-grandchild, and we didn't want her worried while I was pregnant. Instead, I made it a point to visit her and my aunt often so they could see the sonogram pictures of him. I shared funny stories with them about how Junior would twist and turn inside of me, and I loved letting them feel my stomach as he moved around. To me, that was better than inciting worry or fear about the outcome of his health.

My grandmother and aunt were the pillars of my family, and I loved them as much as the day was long. I knew they loved me too. They were so very excited to meet their new family member, and when we all walked into his NICU room, they immediately said, "He's so tiny and so cute!" It was as if they didn't even see all of the tubes that were attached to him, or his head or chin size. All they saw was the newest branch on the family tree, and they were unconditionally in love with him.

And I thought it was so sweet that the nurses had placed the baby-blue, handkerchief-sized blanket that said "Jesus Loves Me" on it near Junior's feet. My grandmother had given it to us at our baby shower, and if there were any item that should have been near him, I was glad it was that. My grandmother got to see her gift in action, which touched her heart as well as mine.

Shortly after we arrived, two doctors came in and told Chris and me that they needed to speak with us. We traveled down a long hallway into a room where they told us our son had kidney issues and no adrenal glands. In addition to that, they were questioning if he had a pituitary gland and a thyroid gland. Before our son was born, the maternal-fetal medicine doctors told us they thought his pituitary and thyroid glands were extremely small; at this point, the doctors who actually specialized in the endocrine system were questioning if our son's glands existed at all. Within his first twenty-four hours of life, an endocrinologist had determined that our son's endocrine system wasn't normal based on results from a post-birth sonogram. She had been administering shots to him, but we didn't know what the shots were for. In this meeting on the second day, the doctors explained to us that those shots were helping to compensate for the hormones that would normally be secreted by his adrenal glands. We had been told that his blood pressure was too low at birth and the doctors were trying to stabilize it, but now we knew why it was so low. He didn't have glands to regulate it. Chris and I figured that if the shots the doctors were giving him were going to help regulate his blood pressure in the hospital, then we would just have to get used to giving him the same shots once we got him home.

After the meeting, my grandmother and my aunt left. They had taken in more information that day than they had ever intended to. They saw how serious our son's condition was. They told us they loved us and would be praying for us.

After we returned to Junior's room, I noticed an extra person was now there, instead of just the doctor and nurse who were there when we left. She introduced herself to me as a respiratory therapist. She explained that she was in charge of all the tubes that were connected to the baby to keep him alive.

At one point, some of his numbers started dropping and the three medical professionals had their eyes locked on the monitors in his room. The doctor in the room turned to me and said, "His numbers are dropping. Do you want to call the chaplain?"

I didn't know what she meant by that, but in the movies I'd seen, when someone was in a person's hospital room and a doctor was asking about a chaplain, it was because the person was going to die. I turned to her with a bit of anger in my voice and asked, "For what?"

She shrugged her shoulders and said, "To pray."

I looked at her and said, "We know how to pray."

The doctors knew we were praying people, but in that moment, I felt like she was asking me about the chaplain almost to mock me.

Maybe I was overly sensitive about it and maybe that's not how she intended for it to come out, but that's how it felt.

Thankfully, Junior's numbers stabilized.

Chris: I left very early to go home, shower, and change my clothes, but I got back to the hospital within a short time because I wanted to make sure I heard everything the doctors said about my son in their morning meeting. I guess because I had grieved hard the night before, Day 2 was easier for me to handle. Right after I arrived at the hospital, a group of doctors gathered outside my son's room. When they talked, it was as if they were speaking in another language that I didn't know. I had no idea what they meant when they spoke, but I stayed attentive.

Following the meeting I was feeling puzzled, and a doctor gently patted my shoulder and asked, "Are you okay?"

I replied, "What the hell did they say?"

He started explaining to me the complexities of my son's condition. I learned that the doctors met in front of every child's room early in the mornings, performing what they called "rounds." It was when doctors discussed the next plan of action for the child.

This day is when I became inquisitive about the various machines Junior was connected to. I noticed there was a screen with lines that were red, white, and blue. I asked the nurse what they meant because they fluctuated regularly. They measured three different things: heart rate, blood pressure, and oxygen. The first thing the hospital was focused on was trying to stabilize Junior's blood pressure. They wanted to wean him off the epinephrine, which was helping with that issue.

At the end of my wife's visit, I took her back to the main hospital and I returned to the children's hospital to spend the day with my son.

It was a quiet evening. My wife had shown me that the uncomfortable couch in Junior's room actually pulled out into a twin-size bed, so that allowed me to sleep peacefully that night.

During the day, like the first day, I met multiple doctors. It was like my boy's room was a museum for doctors. They came in the room, introduced themselves to me, and then viewed the baby.

When the doctors told us they didn't think our son had adrenal glands and that he would have to get shots every day for the rest of his life, I didn't think it was a big deal. When I was first diagnosed with MS, I had to give myself shots every other day; I knew I could help show Junior how to take his shots, too. But what bothered me was that I knew how to breathe to take my shots, and even then, sometimes it hurt when I did it. Junior was a baby, so he didn't know to take a deep breath when it was time to get a shot, and it looked like he was in pain when they gave him shots. I hated seeing my boy like that.

My wife and I didn't really know what adrenal glands did, so we didn't realize how serious it was that our son didn't have them. My wife knew a little bit about the pituitary gland being connected to puberty, so she asked about that, but I had only heard about it. I didn't know what it was for. Based on what the doctors were saying, my boy was a sick baby, and I didn't like calling him sick.

That night when I went home, I knew what I could do to help our situation. I decided make a CD with my voice on it telling my son that he was healthy. I believed in the power of positive thinking, and I was hoping that Junior's subconscious mind would kick in and if he heard that he was healed, he'd actually get healed. On the CD, I spoke the following: "You are the righteousness of God. Your blood pressure is regulated. Your heart rate is regulated. You are the beloved of God. You have the ability to breathe on your own. You are your mother's baby and you are your daddy's boy. And it is so in the name of Jesus."

I wanted the doctors to start playing the CD where he could hear it up by his head twenty-four hours a day. My son was only going to hear what my wife and I had to say about his situation, and we were saying that he was healthy.

+ + +

Thursday, July 23, 2015, 1:05 a.m.

Dear Christopher,

You gave Mommy and Daddy the biggest surprise by showing up early this week! We had no idea that you were going to come on Tuesday, July 21. That will forever be the day when Mommy and Daddy's lives changed. We have enjoyed being able to see you at the hospital, and of course, we are praying for you and believing in God for you. You are a total cutie pie! At this point, we need your health to improve a lot, and we are trusting that He's going to do that. This is a very hard situation for Mommy and Daddy because we love you so much and really want you to get better.

We love you forever and always,

Mommy and Daddy

CHAPTER SEVENTEEN

Day 3:

Friday, July 24, 2015, 12:32 a.m.

Dear Little Boy,

Mommy and Daddy love you so much. It's hard to believe that just a few days ago, you were inside of me. Today was a bit of a rough day for Mommy and Daddy. A lot of doctors talked to us, and they all are trying to determine several things about your little body. Daddy and I continue to pray for you and proclaim that you are healed.

Love you always,

Mommy and Daddy

\+ + +

Chris: I was in full coach mode. I was up early enough to be at the doctors' rounds that morning. I understood that my son's blood pressure was doing incredibly well, so they could begin to decrease and wean him off the epinephrine. My wife's mom was bringing her to the hospital that day, so I could stay with Junior. When she arrived, she heard me cheering for Junior, "Come on, my boy, you're making it." His heart rate numbers were increasing. The nurses as well as my wife were laughing at me, but I was serious because I wanted my son to continue to improve. I had hope that he was coming home. I watched the monitors all day long, and I coached him on what his numbers should be on the monitor. As I told him what he needed to do, it was fun seeing his numbers move in the right direction. I felt like we were making progress.

One of the doctors asked me if there was anything that I especially wanted my boy to have, and I told her I wanted him to get mandibular distraction. In our first big team meeting, the doctors told us he might be a candidate for that because his chin was so small. Since the doctors thought that his chin and airway were small, I thought that if he had a mandibular distraction, it would help him to breathe on his own. I thought that would be the answer to a lot of our problems.

Danielle: On the third day, I was feeling better about our situation. I came to the hospital and started talking to our son, and he opened his eyes and looked up at me. He started moving his head around; it was like he was following my voice. I felt in my heart that these were good signs that he was getting better. Chris was making all of us laugh at his high-pitched imitation of me calling for Junior. And he was repeatedly telling him, "Boy, stop squishing your face up!" We were all laughing and joking, and finally Chris and I were starting to be able to enjoy our little family. But all of this came to an abrupt end when the doctors came and told us they wanted to have a team meeting with us.

My mom was at the hospital that day, and as the doctors led Chris and me out of the room, she asked if we wanted her to go with us. I shook my head. I wanted her to enjoy her time with her new grandbaby, and since we were his parents, I wanted us to hear whatever news they had before anyone else.

Since we'd had a team meeting before, I thought I knew what to expect. I thought the doctors would tell us about the baby's progression and when we could finally take him home.

As Chris and I situated ourselves on a couch in the small room, I started to feel a bit overwhelmed, almost like I did at the first team meeting. The only difference was we already knew some of the doctors in the room this time, because they had been caring for our son.

Neonatologists, neurologists, geneticists, a chaplain, and a palliative care doctor were all in the room. They gave us some good news, but the majority of what they shared with us was bad. They told us that Junior's glucose and blood pressure numbers had improved but that his breathing continued to be a problem for him. They also could tell he had some serious brain abnormalities, but they were confident that they could decrease the fluid from around his brain. Unlike our initial sonogram or even the MRI that helped determine all of his initial issues, the doctors also discovered that he had some genital deformities that hadn't been brought to their attention before. Though it had been mentioned as a one of the possible diagnoses before, the doctors were now more confident that our son had a form of Joubert syndrome, a rare genetic disorder that affects the cerebellum, an area of the brain that controls balance and coordination. The disorder is characterized by the absence or underdevelopment of the cerebellar vermis and a malformed brain stem. If this diagnosis was correct, Junior was going to have severe developmental delays.

They also told us that his bones weren't formed well in his arms and legs. They started telling us all the different procedures they could perform on him, but all of them came with risks, the largest being that he might not actually survive them.

Because of the many severe issues, they weren't sure how much longer Junior would live. They told us they were actually surprised he was still with us. I credited his being alive to our faith in God and His power, Chris speaking life over him, his fighting spirit, and us not giving up on him.

The doctors also told us that if we wanted to, we could choose to turn off the machines that were keeping Junior alive and let him pass away. I felt like the doctors didn't have any more hope for our son. Even though they never said we should let him pass, it was as if they wanted us to realize that that was the best option for our child. But I wouldn't allow myself to give up on our baby now. I mean, just that day he had opened his eyes and looked up at me. He had followed my voice. And in some ways, he was getting better. They had said themselves that his blood pressure and glucose numbers were improving. I didn't want to think about letting him go.

Chris and I sat silently on the couch. They asked what we wanted for our son, and I repeated myself, through sobs and a handful of tissues, "I just want him to get better."

Chris responded, "I don't want him to suffer."

I then gathered enough strength to speak. I had to speak for my baby. I had to fight for him. If I didn't, who would? I was sitting in a room full of medical professionals who I felt like were telling me to let my baby die. "I want my baby to get better," I said, as tears poured down my face. "I just want us to experience good times with him, and I want him to experience a good life. And I've always had these dreams of our child being able to play and run and jump and act like me and his dad, but you're telling me that that isn't possible for this child. And I don't know what to do. I feel like you're telling me to just turn off the machines that are keeping him alive and I don't want to do that. Do I have to do that?"

Our head neonatologist looked over at me and shook his head. "No, you don't have to do that today. But we do want you to understand the severity of Christopher's medical issues," he said as I nodded. "We're not asking you to make any decisions today. We just want you to know what we have seen so far, okay?"

I nodded my head while wiping my face.

"We know you do not want to let your baby go. So why don't we continue to watch him and give him care like we have been giving him. And I think we need to order an MRI to see if we can learn any more information about his total condition, okay?"

I nodded again, still crying, with Chris rubbing my back.

The doctors could tell the meeting had been a bit much for us to handle, and thankfully, our head neonatologist decided to wrap it up. We decided to schedule an MRI for some time later the following week. He told us to go back to spending time with and enjoying our baby.

As they were leaving, one of the palliative care doctors came over to me and kneeled down. She asked me what our son's name was, and I almost didn't have the strength to speak. "Christopher," I mumbled.

"Okay, why don't we start making some memories with Christopher?" It was as if she had turned on my internal faucet and the tears wouldn't stop. She was encouraging me to make memories, but my child was still alive. I didn't want to think about needing to remember him because he wasn't with us. I wanted to go back around the corner to his room, act like that meeting never happened, and move on with our lives. She was suggesting memory making, and I hadn't even had a chance to hold him yet or to nuzzle his cheeks against mine. I know she didn't mean harm by it, but I didn't want to think about memories. I wanted to have experiences with my child.

She got up and left the room as the chaplain came over and grabbed me gently by the shoulder. I was only on a four-hour pass from the hospital, and those doctors had just taken up half of the precious time I could've been spending with our son. (I didn't know the doctors would've let me stay longer if I needed to; I just thought I had to follow the rules.) I sat on the couch in the room with Chris on one side of me and the chaplain on the other, and I bawled uncontrollably. This didn't seem real.

Eventually, we got up and walked back around to our son's room. Chris and I both stood there and stared at our little boy, who we now understood was literally fighting for his life.

I read *Guess How Much I Love You* to our son, just like I had the other nights, and kissed him and told him I loved him.

Chris and I had some very important decisions to make about our son's care.

That night, when I was in the hospital room all by myself, I kept looking at myself in the bathroom mirror. My eyes were bloodshot and my head hurt from crying so much. I didn't know why this was happening to us. I stood in the mirror, looking at myself but talking to God. "Lord, please let our baby live. All I ever wanted was to be a mom. I promise I'll be a good mom," I cried out. "The worst thing I'll do is give him extra ice cream after dinner. That isn't so bad, God. Please…" I walked back over to my bed and climbed in. This pain hurt worse than I ever imagined it would. I thought I had experienced the worst day of my life at our initial team meeting in April, but that didn't compare to how bad this day had been. It was a new low.

My dad called me, and had it been anyone else, I wouldn't have answered the phone. I didn't really want to answer the phone even for him, but he was my dad. I felt compelled to. "Hello," I whispered, exhausted from crying.

"Hey, baby girl, it's Daddy. I'm just calling to check on you," he said.

"Hi, Daddy." I was uncharacteristically short and quiet.

"Are you okay?" he asked me.

"No."

He paused and then responded, "Do you want to talk about it?"

I replied, "No."

My dad and I are the quintessential dad/daughter duo. I am my daddy's little girl and I always will be no matter how old I get. Growing up, he was the first man who told me he loved me; he was the first man who complimented me. He was the first man to wish me a Happy Valentine's Day. He disciplined me and corrected me yet always let me know I could come to him for help. We had an unbreakable bond. I loved my daddy, and my daddy loved me. He had been to the hospital to see his grandson, and over the last several months, he and I talked about all of the issues that the doctors were saying the baby had. So when he asked me if I wanted to talk about my problems, I even surprised myself when I told him no. This wasn't something I wanted to talk to anyone about. This wasn't something that anyone could help me with. This was something that was just going to have to "be."

Chris: That night, I went back to my wife's hospital room and sat down on the couch. We didn't know what to think. She was crying and I was still trying to understand what the doctors meant when they talked to us earlier in the day. They didn't give us an ultimatum, and we still had a little bit of the "wait and see" hope for improvement, but that was starting to dwindle. I felt like my wife was taking this news very, very hard. This was my boy they were talking about. I was still holding out hope that he would get better.

Danielle and I talked, and we weren't sure what to do. I was still believing that my boy's health would improve, even though it didn't look good. To me, it seemed like his biggest issue was his airway being blocked. I thought if I could push for the mandibular distraction, which would push his chin out, he would at least be able to breathe. But the doctors never really moved forward on that issue. I also asked them about him getting a tracheostomy if he couldn't get the mandibular distraction, but they told us that there were other issues that came along with tracheostomies and they didn't think that would be the best plan for our son.

I felt like there wasn't much else I could do that night for my family. But to do something positive, since his blood pressure was getting regulated, I decided to make another healing CD. This time when I recorded my voice, I took the part about his blood pressure out, since there was no need to leave it in there. I continued to tell Junior that he was loved.

+ + +

July 24, 2015, 11:34 p.m.—three days old!
Dear Little Boy,

Today you opened your eyes for Mommy and Daddy. Yay! I really, really love you. Mommy and Daddy, some of your aunties, and your grandma came to visit you today. We had a really good visit with you. You held our hands, opened your eyes, responded to Mommy's voice, and moved around. You are so cute! The doctors have told us that you are a sick baby, but Daddy and I are still believing that you are going to get healthy. God gave you to us as a gift, and no matter what, we are going to cherish you forever. Before anyone else knew you, Mommy knew you, and you will always be her baby. Her little boy. Keep on getting better! Mommy and Daddy love you so much. Daddy has spent more time with you than anyone. He's a great dad and he loves you so much. He's spent the night with you at the hospital, made you a healing CD, and brags about you wherever he goes. You are his world!

We love you,
Mommy and Daddy

CHAPTER EIGHTEEN

Days 4 and 5:

Chris: For two days, we got to spend all day with our boy. My oldest brother came to visit with us at the hospital, and it was good having him there. My parents had come a couple of times earlier in the week to check on Junior and to check on me and my wife, and that felt good. I was proud that I had made my new healing CD, and the doctors and nurses made sure to play it during the day for Junior. I felt like it was helping the situation. I just wanted my boy to get better.

Danielle: I was discharged from the hospital on Day 4, which meant I could spend the whole day with Chris and the baby, which I was really looking forward to. I didn't have to worry about only being on a four-hour visitor pass. Up until that point, Chris had been spending almost twelve hours a day at the hospital with our son, and now I could too. I know that may have seemed like a long time to some people, but to us, we cherished each and every moment of it.

That weekend, Chris and I joked around with the nurses and had them laughing with our shenanigans. We told them Junior's worst problem would be having us as parents!

I finally thought I'd be able to hold the baby and cuddle with him, but his numbers didn't stabilize, so it still didn't happen. But on the bright side, some of my closest girlfriends whom I've known for almost my whole life came to visit with us, and it was wonderful having them at the hospital. They listened to us, laughed with us, brought us gifts, and let us know they loved us.

Day 6:

Chris: My wife finally had an opportunity to hold our son, and I was so happy for her. I knew being in my wife's arms was going to help Junior get better. I really believe that mothers have healing power within their bodies for their children. It was good seeing her get excited, and I even recorded the nurses putting the baby into her arms.

Danielle: The day I'd been looking forward to had finally come! I got a chance to hold my baby. It was a production, though. Any time the doctors or nurses moved him, he had to have at least two people carrying him, and one of those people had to be a respiratory therapist. And once he was in my arms, I had to stay as still as possible. I loved every single minute of holding our baby boy. I got to sing to him and rub his cheeks and kiss him. That was by far the best day of us being in the hospital. Plus, my brother came to visit, and he got a chance to meet his little nephew. He was super excited about officially being an uncle.

Day 7:

Chris: When my wife and I walked into my boy's room, the lights were dimmed and he was under a blue light because of his jaundice. I thought that the little goggles they had on him were funny, but the doctors said they were there to protect his eyes. A few days before that, the eye doctor came to see him and he told us he thought Junior could see out of his left eye but not out of his right eye.

The doctors scheduled our son to have his first MRI done at a week old, and my wife and I wanted to be with him when he was going through his first major medical test.

That night, my wife and I were watching our son from the NICview camera and we saw that the goggles had come off. My wife called the NICU and asked one of the nurses to put the googles back on. She told us she did, but when we viewed the footage on the NICview camera again, we realized she hadn't. I was upset because I didn't want his eyes to get damaged. I told my wife we were going to the hospital so I could do it myself.

We got to the hospital that night around 11 p.m., and when I was walking into my boy's room, the nurse saw me and hurried into the room before me. She told me that maybe the goggles had come back off accidentally. I was glad that we went to the hospital to check on my boy. I wanted the nurses to know we were serious about our son.

+ + +

Tuesday, July 28, 2015, 5:40 p.m.

Dear Little Boy,

Today you are one week old! This past week has been a roller coaster. Mommy and Daddy have been with you every day at the hospital. We want to make sure you are well taken care of. Your nurses are all so nice and we like them. You've had some good days and we are so proud of you. You are a fighter! Mommy's stubbornness and Daddy's stubbornness are paying off for you. You have it honestly. Yesterday, I was able to hold you for the first time! Yay! Your nurse said that when you were in my arms that was the best you'd been. I like holding your hand, kissing your cheeks and neck, and loving on you! Yesterday, you jaundiced, so today the doctors put you under the blue lights to help you. Mommy and Daddy truly love you with our whole heart. We just want you to get better soon. We love you sooo much.

Love always,

Mommy and Daddy

CHAPTER NINETEEN

Day 8:

Danielle: My husband told me we needed to stay home at least one day, and although I wanted to stay at the hospital every day with the baby, I was glad we ended up getting some rest for ourselves. That morning, when the nurse called to tell us how our son was doing, I asked her to explain the different numbers the doctors rattled off each morning in their rounds. I made little flashcards with the information that she gave us so we'd be ready the next morning to understand exactly what the doctors were saying. And the nurse told us that our son's MRI results would be ready the next morning. We felt like we'd finally get some answers.

That night, I needed more bottles to continue pumping my milk, plus I just couldn't stay away from the baby. I asked Chris if we could make a late-night hospital run so we could tell him goodnight.

\+ + +

Thursday, July 30, 2015, 12:31 a.m.

Dear Junior,

Mommy and Daddy love you so much! I didn't write in your book yesterday, but you had to be under blue lights all day long because you were jaundiced the day before. You looked like a little space cadet with the blue lights and your little goggles. Mommy and Daddy watch you all the time on the NICview cameras and if we see something that we don't like, we call your nurses. Well, last night, Daddy noticed that your goggles to protect your eyes from the photo therapy (blue light) weren't on. Daddy called the nurse three times and told her to cover your eyes. After she didn't do it the way your daddy wanted, we drove to the hospital so Daddy could put them on you. The night before that, Mommy was watching the camera and noticed that it looked like you needed to be suctioned. Mommy called the nurse three or four times and the nurse finally did what I asked her to do. Those doctors and nurses are finding out how serious we are about your care! We have a team meeting tomorrow and I pray it goes well. I love you and so does Daddy!

Day 9:

Danielle: That morning I felt great. We had a chance to sleep in the day before, and we were well rested. I felt so refreshed and ready to go to the hospital to find out about our son's MRI. I was ready to hear good news, and I was ready to love on our son. Plus, I had contacted a good friend of mine who was a doctor at the hospital who saw medically complex patients. I asked her if she'd be willing to attend the meeting with us just to translate some of the "doctor-speak." I didn't know if maybe I hadn't quite understood everything that the doctors told us in the first meeting, or maybe I just didn't want to. But having a trusted doctor there with us for the meeting couldn't hurt.

Shortly after we started visiting with our son, the doctors let us know they were ready to meet with us. We went to the same room where we had been just a week prior. But this time around, I felt like we would be able to handle whatever news they were going to give us.

The doctor started this meeting like they had started others, by asking us what we wanted for our son. Our answers were still the same.

"I'm his mama. I just want my baby to get better," I said.

"I don't want my boy to suffer," Chris said, as he had so many times before.

The doctors started going around the circle, explaining to us that our son's condition was not improving. In addition to everything they had already told us, the MRI confirmed that his brain was completely abnormal and, as suspected, he had none of his glands, which were essential to living. The mandibular distraction that Chris had so desperately desired was no longer an option for our son.

The doctors then broke the most devastating news to us. Our son's brain stem was severely, abnormally underdeveloped. The brain stem is essential to being alive. Parts of it control the cardiac, respiratory, heart rate, breathing, and blood pressure functions of the body. The condition of his brain stem helped explain all the issues we had seen in Junior since he was born. While he was inside of me, his heart rate was regulated because I was helping to regulate it. But when he was outside of me and had to do it on his own, it wasn't possible. It was almost like watching a kid who wanted so badly to do something but just couldn't do it. After learning all of this, the doctors were impressed that our son had been doing as well as he had and so were we.

The doctors made it very clear to us what our choices were. We could leave our son hooked up to all the machines in the hospital and request that the doctors start doing some of the medical procedures they had discussed, such as the brain shunt and the omphalocele correction. We could choose to start prepping our son to come home with us, still being connected to all the machines that were keeping him alive. Or we, as his parents, could make the decision to turn off the machines and let Junior go live with Jesus.

None of those options sounded good. I sat on the couch unable to move.

Chris: "So you're telling me my son is going to be a vegetable?" I asked the doctor.

"I can't say that, because that is not an official medical term, but..." the doctor said while nodding his head up and down to signal yes.

My heart sank, but I wasn't ready to give up on my boy. "I know my wife wants to take our son to Disney World," I said. "But would he know that he's there?"

The doctor shook his head no.

"Okay, I know you all keep saying that he has an airway issue. What would happen if you used an inhaler on him? Would that open up his airway so he can breathe?"

The doctor sat at the edge of his chair and shook his head. "But that was good thinking. Do you have any other suggestions?" the doctor asked, smiling at me.

"No. But tell me this: If we take our son home, can he still die even if he's connected to all of those machines?"

The doctor nodded and answered, "Yes."

"Aw, man," I let out a sigh and sat back into the couch.

The doctor was very straightforward. "We could perform two hundred procedures on this baby and none of them would help him. It is his brain stem that is causing these issues. There is nothing to help that," he told us. "We want to help you, but there is nothing more we can do. So you, sir, are saying you don't want to allow him to suffer. You now need to decide what you and your wife want to do. Do you want to put him through a ton of surgeries that are not going to help him? If not, what do you want us to do so we can move forward and make sure that he is comfortable? If his heart stops while he is still in the hospital, what do you want us to do? We do not see him getting any better. His prognosis is that he will be on a feeding tube, a suction machine, and a ventilator for the rest of his life."

Danielle: After hearing the doctor say the baby could still die at home while being connected to the machines, which seemed like the equivalent of having a hospital at home, I felt like there was nothing else we could do. I thought for a split second that maybe we should try to hold on for a little bit longer, but as the tears rolled slowly down my cheeks, I had to swallow the painful reality that we were going to have to let our son go.

Chris, my doctor friend, and I walked back around the corner to our son's room, where all seven pounds and eight ounces of him lay connected to machines. The doctors had presented their case to us, and none of our options was good. And now we had to make the decision over what we wanted to do regarding our son's life. As we walked in, we had heard Chris's voice softly coming across the CD player he had placed near our son's head so he could hear his daddy's voice.

After the door shut behind us, Chris all but yelled, "I can't believe God would do this!" He had tears in his eyes and his voice was shaking. He shook his fists and paced back and forth across the hospital room, and then he stormed out. I decided it was probably best to give him some alone time. This was hard on both of us. I had carried our son for almost nine months and he had heard my voice and listened to my heartbeat and had gotten all he needed while he was inside me. But once he came out of me, his daddy had spent the most time with him and hardly ever left his side. Chris was the one who had stood by his son's bed for hours on end, coaching him on how to do the basics of life. He was the one who was adamant about saying only positive things around him, and he would never utter the word "sick" when he was talking about his son's medical condition. Junior was Chris's best friend, as he often referred to him. Junior made his daddy proud.

I sat down in the rocking chair in our son's room where I had held him for the first time three days prior. My doctor friend pulled up a chair and sat across from me. She took me by the hands and looked into my eyes. "Danielle, not just as a doctor, but as your friend, everything they are saying is correct. It is not going to get better," she said softly as I began to weep.

"So, you mean to tell me that you see patients who are eighteen and twenty years old but have the mental capacity of a baby?"

Still holding my hands and looking at me, she replied, "Yes. And it is a very hard life on them and their parents."

I put my head down and let the tears flow. I knew what our decision needed to be, but I didn't want to make that decision. But all our options led to the same sad outcome.

Chris returned to the room with swollen red eyes, and our doctor friend said she would give us some time to ourselves. She offered to buy dinner for us that night and told us she would check on us before she left work that evening.

Chris and I stood silently for a few minutes. And then both of us were crying. "What if we make the decision to turn off all the machines and you take your shirt off and lay him on your chest? We can see if your body somehow will regulate his heartbeat," Chris proposed.

I nodded. "Okay," I said.

"We gotta give him a chance to breathe on his own, otherwise he's never going to do it."

"You're right," I told him.

Chris told the nurse that we had made our decision regarding what we wanted to do and she got the doctor.

It hadn't been an hour since our team meeting when our head neonatologist came back into our room. "What did you decide?" he asked.

Chris told him our plan of turning off the machines and finally allowing me to have one-on-one, chest-to-chest contact with our baby boy, in hopes that something positive would change in his little body.

"And when do you want to do this?" the doctor asked.

"We want to do it tomorrow at 5 p.m."

The doctor asked one final question, "If he starts gasping for air when we take the breathing tube out and turn the machines off, do you want us to resuscitate him?"

I almost said yes, but my better judgment prevailed. Chris and I looked at each other and responded the same away: "No."

"Okay," the doctor said. "We will follow your wishes."

Chris and I decided that if we let the baby lie on my chest and he started to breathe, we would put him back into his bed, knowing that at least he was breathing on his own. But if he did not, we knew Jesus would be welcoming him with open arms and he would finally be at peace. Besides, there were no X-rays, MRIs, needle pricks, monitors, blood transfusions, IVs, feeding tubes, ventilators, or any other medical equipment in heaven. Plus, there was infinite space for a little boy on the move.

The rest of that day was bittersweet. The children's hospital's child life person on the NICU floor made molds of our son's hands and feet, and she took his handprints and footprints. When it was time for her to take our hand molds, our precious baby boy wouldn't let our fingers go. So instead of us just having molds of his hands, we have molds of him holding onto our hands. I got to hold our son again for as long as I wanted, and while doing so, I read books to him and kissed him all over. Up until that point, Chris had really wanted to make sure that I had a chance to hold him, but on that day, I wanted to make sure he had a chance to hold him too. I didn't want him to regret not holding his boy and best friend. So he held him and got to tell him face to face, big man to little boy, that he was his daddy's boy. It was funny how a person who was so adamant about not wanting to have kids had grown so attached in such a strong way to this little person. It's amazing how a child can completely change his parents.

That night, as I'd done so many times before, I read *Guess How Much I Love You* to our little boy. I placed special emphasis on "I love you to the moon and back." I'd always meant it, but that night I really, really meant it.

That night at the hospital, our doctor friend returned and my best friend visited with us. As I sat rocking Junior, I rambled, trying to make sense of what was happening, even though at the time, it seemed senseless. "Maybe God is going to use him in some great way to help a lot of other people," I said, with Junior's head clutched underneath my chin and his little arm resting on my chest. "Maybe there's another child out there that has something that he has and his whole purpose was to just come here to help someone else out." They both sat quietly and listened, not saying much but just being good friends.

Chris and I knew we wanted our son's life to serve a great purpose, and initially we thought he was going to be a miracle child who defied all of the odds and went on to live a healthy life. But that night, that miracle didn't seem within reach. We started to think how we could possibly help other families in the midst of what we were going through.

I had known about being able to donate breast milk because I'd worked so closely with the milk bank center at the children's hospital. When we made our decision to turn off our son's machines that were keeping him alive, I immediately got in touch with the lactation consultant who worked in the NICU. I told her about my decision, and she helped me every step of the way. I ended up pumping milk for six weeks, and in that brief time, I donated more than three thousand feedings' worth of milk to babies at seven different NICUs across three different states.

Chris and I had agreed that Junior should be an organ donor, and the child life staff called in someone from the local organ donor network. But when the representative arrived, he told us sadly that because of Junior's congenital abnormalities, he couldn't be a live organ donor. But then I remembered my little brother who had passed away and how my parents courageously donated his organs to research. By donating Junior's organs to research, doctors would be able to continue studying what caused him to be so sick in the first place. We told our doctors we wanted to donate all of the organs that could be donated in hopes that they would help scientists in their work. We eventually learned that our son's brain, brain stem, lungs, and heart were all being used to help researchers.

Chris reminded me that he had consented for our son to be a part of different research studies while he was in the hospital. In fact, for one of the studies, Junior was the first patient enrolled. And we had given his doctors permission to talk about him and to write about him in journals and publications as they saw necessary. We wanted other families to be helped by our child. We were still believing in a miracle, even on that night, but if our child happened to pass away the next day, we knew he was going to be a world changer, even in his death.

+ + +

Friday, July 31, 2015, 12:14 a.m.

Dear Little Boy,

Mommy and Daddy are sad…very sad. We want you to get better, but it doesn't seem to be happening that way. So today we made peace with the fact that you may not live very much longer. And we are okay with that. Very sad about it but okay with it. Mommy and Daddy are very proud of you because you have been a champ the entire time. You have fought a good fight and have made Mommy and Daddy so proud. If you end up leaving this earth, it would be way too soon for Mommy and Daddy, but we know that God has a purpose and a plan for everything. Little Boy, we love you to the moon and back. We are truly trusting God with you. He can do a way better job than we ever could.

We love you soooo much, xoxo,

Mommy and Daddy

CHAPTER TWENTY

Day 10:

Danielle: To my surprise, we actually rested well going into July 31. But when I woke up that morning, I went into the room that our son would not be coming home to, and I broke down. I decided to hang two of his jerseys on his bed. One said "Daddy's co-pilot" and one said "Mommy's little guy." Chris and I both loved Junior immensely. He would never have had to worry about whether his parents cared about him. Hanging both of these jerseys was a way to honor both my love for Junior and Chris's love for our son. Chris and I were a team in everything—even in this horrible situation we didn't want to face. As I was hanging his jerseys, emotion overwhelmed me. I found myself with my forehead resting on the bar of Junior's crib and my arms outstretched across it. I lay there wailing and screaming. I could not believe that "this" was actually happening. We had held onto faith, we had prayed, we had believed, we had spoken good things, we made sure we were healthy. We did everything we knew to do to have a healthy child, and this was happening.

I was glued to our baby's crib. My husband came in and tried to comfort me, but I was inconsolable. He tried his hardest, all while still being gentle, to get me to return to our bedroom, but I would not. I could not. Finally, after I felt like I'd gotten everything out, I walked back into our bedroom slowly and lay in the bed next to my husband. This did not feel good.

That morning I decided to call my family and let them know what was happening. There was no way I could let our baby boy pass away without letting them know about it. I needed them praying for us throughout the day. As I made my calls one by one to the same group of people who had received little Christmas gifts from their new family member, I had to tell them he was returning home to Jesus. While they were all sad, they understood our decision and promised to be there for us in the days to come. I was comforted by knowing that they had all come to the hospital over the last ten days to see our little guy. He'd had a chance to meet some of the most important people ever.

Chris had decided to wait until later that night to contact his family. He would let them know in his own way what was going on.

That day, I called my pastor's wife and pastor to see if they would stop by the hospital to pray with us one final time for our miracle. They had been believing with us since the night of our first team meeting, and they were still believing with us. It was good having them there to support us however this day would turn out.

Two of the geneticists who had been working on our son's case met with us that morning. We asked them a lot of questions and wanted to know if there was anything at all they could do to help us. We were open to any ideas they had, but unfortunately, they had none. They pulled up pictures of what a normal baby's brain stem looked like, and they put it next to a picture of our baby's brain stem. There was no comparison. Our son's brain stem wasn't formed all the way.

The medical team made sure to call a photography service that takes remembrance pictures of families who have lost or are about to lose their infant children. Chris and I wanted to have family photos, and with the help of this photographer, we would. We hadn't brought any of Junior's clothes from home, but the NICU had a special reserve of new clothes for babies, and I had picked out an outfit I thought was super cute. And as a special touch and a way to honor Chris, I even picked out a bib that had "Handsome Like Daddy" across it. It reminded me of the ones Chris picked out the day we registered for our baby items.

Chris and I got the baby dressed, and my pastor's wife and the nurse helped direct us. All of us in the room couldn't stop laughing as Chris shimmied Junior down into his little pants like a little sack of potatoes. Leave it to Chris to keep us laughing on the day our son was passing away.

Five o'clock had come and gone, but I just wasn't ready yet to say good-bye. Plus, the photographer hadn't arrived until around 4:30, and I wanted to make sure I spent as much time as I wanted to with our son on his last day on earth. I didn't want to have any regrets about not holding him long enough (which was already limited), not kissing or hugging him long enough, not whispering in his ears long enough, or not telling him I loved him enough. Every second and every minute of that day was precious to me.

Finally, right before 7 p.m., I was ready for God to either perform one of the greatest miracles ever and cause our son to breathe on his own, or I was ready for Him to welcome our son into His arms. With Chris, me, a neonatologist, the photographer, a nurse, and a child life specialist being the only people in the room, it was time. The neonatologist asked us one final time, "If he gasps for air after we take this tube out, do you want us to resuscitate him?"

"No," we answered in unison.

The doctors told us that when our son was born, he'd had to be resuscitated three times and the tube that was down his throat allowing him to live was forced. We weren't going to put him through that kind of trauma again. Plus, the doctors had administered pain medication to him so he wouldn't suffer and his transition would be peaceful.

The medical professionals took the tube out of his mouth, and for the first time since the moment he was born, I was able to see my baby boy's face with no medical equipment attached to it. I got a chance to really examine him and to study his little nose and chin and all of his little chunky baby rolls. I got a chance to whisper to him and tell him I loved him and that we were proud of him. The whole day I had been singing a song that I had only heard once before. It talked about how even in the midst of life's storms, a person could still have peace. I held on tightly to my baby boy, to our baby boy, and I had peace.

Several times over the course of me holding our son that night, Chris whispered into my ear two very clear messages through his own heartache and tears: "We will not let this tear us apart—we will stay together through this," and "We are making the right decision."

The neonatologist frequently checked Junior's heart to see if it was still beating, and at 7:23 p.m., on Friday, July 31, our baby went to live with Jesus.

I had greatly desired to hold my baby, and when it was all said and done, I'd been able to hold him only on days 6, 9, and 10 of his life.

After he passed away, we put him back into his bed and the nurse let me give him a bath. It was something I hadn't been able to do before because of the tubes that were in him. And to think, I had just bought a bunch of extra bath wash and lotion for him the Sunday before he was born; now he wouldn't even be able to use it. I found it within me to make a few jokes with the medical staff, and I thanked them for their care. The neonatologist who was with us that night was the same doctor who had asked me on Day 2 if I'd wanted to call a chaplain. She apologized to me if she came across the wrong way, but she told me from her heart that she honestly hadn't known if our son was going to make it through the night. In fact, all of the doctors were surprised he had lived as long as he did.

After giving Junior a bath, I swaddled him tightly in a blanket for the first and last time and bent over and kissed his lifeless body. We had done what any good parents would have done. We believed the best for our child with everything that we had in us, and we had done everything we had known to do to show our faith in action. Our son may have died that night, but no one would ever be able to take away our faith, the fact that he was our child, and the fact that we were his parents.

Chris: At the hospital that night, my main thought was, "Let's get this over with." I just wanted it all to end so I didn't have to feel the pain of my son dying. Maybe I was just trying to ignore the facts, but that night before the doctors took the tube out of Junior, I told my wife, "I don't think he's going to die. I think he's going to be okay." I was doing whatever I could not to face what was going to happen.

When they took the tubes out of him, I cried and cried. And I kept on saying, "I thought I was ready for this, but I wasn't." I laid my head on my wife's shoulder when she held him, and I felt so bad for him because he was suffocating, but he didn't know he was suffocating due to the medicines he was on. In that moment, I thought about how God sees us going through life hurting, even when we don't realize we're hurting.

As I watched my wife hold our son for the last time, I was rejoicing yet also felt extremely sad. My boy could finally be consoled by the love I wanted him to have from his mother.

Danielle: As we were leaving the NICU that night, a woman coming in asked me, "Are you leaving with your baby today?"

With all of the stuff in my arms, I did look like I was leaving with something, but I wasn't leaving with my baby. "No," I politely told her as Chris wheeled me onto the elevator and down to the car.

As the neonatologist helped us out to the car, she thanked us for letting her and the team of doctors take care of our son. She told us they had learned so much from us and from our family and that they were inspired by our faith. But she also told us something that I had never considered before: "Your child was loved every single day of his life, and not everyone can say that." Her words pierced my soul. She was right. Our little guy may have departed this earthly life, but while he was here, he was certainly loved.

As she walked away, there was what seemed to be a family at the front of the hospital in front of a dark-colored car. There was a teenager in a wheelchair who appeared to be disabled, and the family was trying as hard as they could to figure out what to move over and how to move it over and how to rearrange everyone in the car to fit the teenager in. We are not people to judge, but for a quick second we caught a glimpse of what our lives could have been like if Junior had come home with us. As hard as it was for us to acknowledge, Chris turned to me and said, "We made the right decision." I agreed with him, got in the car, and we left the hospital.

That night I learned many lessons regarding caring for a loved one who has severe challenges. There is no standard right or wrong decision for any family who has to make choices when it comes to end of life, comfort care, or even how to care for a family member with severe special needs. All a family can do is make the best decision based on the information they have and on what they believe is right for their family.

Driving away, I was numb from what had happened, and I still couldn't make sense of it. On top of all of that, I felt alone. I had my husband right next to me and we were going to meet my parents for dinner, but I felt alone. I couldn't believe our son had actually died.

CHAPTER TWENTY-ONE

Danielle: The next morning, it was as if the wind had been knocked out of me by a ton of bricks. I was numbed by our circumstances. We were parents, but we weren't. We had a child, but he wasn't alive. We had everything at home prepared for a baby to live with us, but we weren't bringing a baby home. What in the world was this?

That morning, we went to the BMV because we needed to get permanent plates for the vehicle we had just purchased for our growing family. While standing in line and making small talk with the man in front of us, he asked if I was pregnant. I told him no and that I had just had a baby. He had no idea that the baby died, and I didn't expect him to. And at that point, the baby had passed away less than eighteen hours before, such a short time ago for me to start referring to our son in past tense. The man continued to engage us in conversation. He told us about how fun it was to raise little boys and how they were like little kings. He had no idea what we had been through, but Chris and I just nodded and smiled along with him, never really saying much.

After we left the BMV, I reached out to a few friends on social media who I knew had lost children before. "Feeling alone" wasn't a good feeling; I needed someone praying for us who understood what this felt like. I was also at the point where I felt comfortable telling more of our family and friends that our son had passed away. I was still a little ashamed that we had made the decision to take our son off life support. I was thinking that people would probably judge us or talk badly about us. But if they were in our situation, I was almost certain they would've made the same decision. Chris and I kept thinking about if we had brought our son home, hooked up to all of the machines, and he passed away in the middle of the night. That would've been devastating to us. We would much rather him pass away in a safe environment surrounded by medical professionals who had cared for him.

Chris: Right after my boy passed away, I had a lot of questions for God, like "Why?" "Why did You allow this to happen?" It was well within His power to snap His fingers and make our son healthy. Right after Junior died, I had a couple of hours when I was mad, when I was questioning God. I wanted to turn away from Him, but my heart wouldn't let me. What got me through that time was that I kept praying, kept thinking about it, and kept remembering that God's decisions are perfect. And He is perfect. And even if my son passed away, it was still a perfect decision.

From talking with my brother, I concluded that even though my wife gave birth to this child, he didn't belong to us, he belonged to God, and He was going to do whatever He wanted with his life. It helped me to put things this way. I think it would've been more detrimental if I didn't believe in God or if I didn't have any explanation, but God allowing this to happen gave me an explanation.

Danielle: The Sunday after our son passed away, I found myself feeling the way I had on the day we learned that our son had several medical issues. I wanted to be around people who were praising God and where I could do the same. I told Chris I wanted to go to church, and he gladly took me to the church I had called home for the last two years. We sat in the back of the sanctuary and were quiet for the majority of the service. By that time, people had started learning that our son had passed away. We were met with tight hugs and people checking in on us once the service was over.

After church, we went to Chris's oldest brother and sister-in-law's house just to relax and to spend time with them. We knew we had a long road ahead, and our families knew we would need their support along the way. While there, our almost three- and six-year-old nieces had a lot of questions for us. They knew we were expecting a baby, and they were really excited to become big cousins, almost like big sisters since we spent so much time with them. But when Junior died, their mom gently explained as best she could that the baby had passed away. But smart kids have good questions, and I don't think Chris or I were ready to answer them.

"Auntie, what happened to the baby?"

"Well, he went to go live with Jesus," I replied.

"Well, why did he go live with Jesus? Why did he die?" they wanted to know.

And honestly, I wanted to know too. "He was sick," I told them.

"Well, why was he sick? Did he have a boo-boo, Auntie?"

How in the world was I supposed to explain this to them? I hadn't even thought about having to explain our new normal to kids. As I was thinking of a response, they noticed I had a picture of him on my phone.

"Can we see his picture, Auntie? He's so cute!"

This was going to be a long day. Using a tactic that so many adults had used on me when I was a kid, I decided to divert their attention. "Why don't you girls go play upstairs?" I was exhausted from that three-minute conversation, and I didn't have many answers for them.

If answering a bunch of questions about what happened to the baby was in my future, I wasn't sure what I was going to do.

That Monday, Chris started the new job he had been offered only two weeks prior. It didn't matter if it was temporary or not, and it may have not been the best thing emotionally to do, but at the time he really wanted to go back to work. He was looking forward to starting at a new place. And during that week, we began to tell more people about our son passing away. We had decided not to have a funeral. Honestly, I don't know if we would've been able to make it through the service. Chris had only been through a handful of funerals before in his whole life, and for me, the experience of holding my baby in my arms as he took his last breaths was draining enough. We instead decided to have our son cremated, so we could officially bring him home with us in a small urn that would be placed inside of a teddy bear. After picking up the bear from the funeral home, I strapped it into Junior's car seat just as the car seat technician had showed me to do for Junior. Technically, I was still transporting him home, and I wanted to make sure he was safe while he rode. And though I wasn't able to dress my real baby, I could dress the teddy bear that served as his final resting place. So, I found cute teddy bear outfits and figured I'd rotate them during the months. The one Chris and I both liked the most was none other than a little Bengals jersey and shorts set, complete with a helmet and football.

The amount of support we received in the weeks that followed was truly amazing. People brought us dinner; the sent us grocery, gas, and restaurant gift cards, money, and small gifts. If we ever needed to know we were loved, we found out that week.

The support and well-wishes from our loved ones didn't stop with gift cards and gifts. Within days of our son passing away, my coworkers wanted to know what they could do to honor his life via monetary donations. That brought tears to my eyes. Chris and I couldn't think of a better place for people to donate to other than the children's hospital NICU. In all of my years working at that children's hospital, being there with Junior was my first truly personal, long-time patient family experience. How blessed was I to be able to experience the superb care I had written about for so many years? Every doctor, nurse, and medical professional who had taken care of our son had done so with such great compassion. And they had taken great care of us too. Why not have people donate money to the NICU's general fund where it could possibly be used to help purchase another NICview camera so parents could watch their ill babies from home, as Chris and I had done so many times? Or maybe the money would be used to help buy more baby clothes for the infants, like the ones Junior had worn in his first and last set of family pictures with us. Perhaps the donations could help buy meal cards for families who didn't want to leave the hospital for food because they wanted to be near their baby. Maybe the money could buy some of the materials like the child life specialist used to make the hand molds and footprints we now had to cherish our baby. Perhaps the money could purchase disposable bottles for the lactating moms like me who weren't able to feed their babies their own milk because of a medical situation. Or maybe the money could be used to purchase other medical supplies the NICU needed to help families. I loved that my coworkers wanted to donate, and I was proud that Chris and I had selected a cause that was near and dear to our hearts.

SPRING

"The promise of spring's arrival is enough to get anyone through the bitter winter."

—Jen Selinksy

CHAPTER TWENTY-TWO

By October, Junior had been gone from us for only three months. All of the giving back we had been able to do and initiate felt so good. But even with everything that had happened, I still believed in my heart that more goodness was ahead. I just didn't know what.

I had already joined an advisory board that was working to help reduce infant mortality within our city, and Chris and I agreed to let them use our story in their annual report and to do some public speaking at events for them. I also got more involved on the board for the only full-time children's hospice program in our region, where I could lend the voice of a bereaved parent. And Chris and I shared our story with the local fetal infant mortality review program, which helps improve systems and services to people who have endured child loss. We had even done an interview with a news station about our story as a way to bring attention to Perinatal and Infant Loss Awareness Month.

I returned to work ten weeks after Junior passed away, and it felt great being back around my coworkers. It was nice getting back into the swing of things. And just like my coworkers had put pictures of their children on their desks, on my first day back I put up my own. One was a picture of Junior from the first time I had ever held him; two others were of me, Chris, and Junior—our perfect little happy family.

The doctors were finally able to give us two essential pieces of information that we so desperately longed for. One was Junior's autopsy report. Not to our surprise, the ultimate cause of his death was his abnormal brain stem and all of the other congenital abnormalities he had. They were also able to tell us what he passed away from. Even though we were adamant about not having genetic testing done when we were initially asked, after we learned (and truly understood) that it would lead to answers for us regarding why he passed away, we agreed to it. And we were glad we did. As it turns out, Junior had an extremely rare genetic condition. After his death, doctors were able to run extensive tests on Junior, Chris, and me. We learned that Junior's OFD1 gene on the 515th panel of his X-chromosome was defective. That one gene caused all of the other problems in his little body. And it happened at the point of conception. Neither Chris nor I knew about the defect before Junior was born, and our little fighter was doing everything he knew to live through it. The doctors knew we were people of faith, and one of them told us that everyone had genes and those genes are what make all of us different. God had just chosen to map Junior's genes differently.

I found it very hard to take in this information, because I felt like I was Mary who had given birth to a modern-day Jesus. I wasn't being sacrilegious; I knew my child wasn't the Savior of the world, nor was I making an equal comparison. But I knew that Mary's child was born so he could die to help a lot of people, some He knew and some He did not. Our son's entire being, everything he was and everything he was to become, was purposed to help other people. And as a mother grieving her child, that hurt a lot.

It also hurt when I found out that I was the carrier of the gene defect that our son had been given. Because the gene defect occurred on Junior's X-chromosome, that meant he had gotten it from me. I was comforted when doctors told me that although he may have gotten it from me, I did not cause it. As Chris and I continued to acknowledge, we got our genetics from God. God was the One who decided for Junior to have the defect, and He chose us for it to happen to. That belief helped us get through the death of our son.

The doctors told us that when it came to us getting pregnant again, we should go through in vitro fertilization (IVF) to ensure that the same thing didn't happen again. After running the tests, they discovered that when it came to medical statistics, if we conceived again naturally with a little boy, there would be a 50/50 chance that the same thing could happen that happened with Junior because the genetic defect is fatal for boys. If we conceived again naturally with a little girl, there was a 25 percent chance she could be a carrier for the genetic defect, like me. If we were to go through IVF with an additional procedure known as preimplantation genetic diagnosis (PGD), the scientists would be able to test our embryos and impregnate me only with the ones that didn't have any trace of the genetic defect that Junior had. It would be the best way of making sure we didn't go through what we had with Junior.

Around the same time, I got discouraged about how life had gone for us. I cried so hard one day in my bathroom, and I just wanted it all to end. It seemed like we had been through so many devastating circumstances in such a short amount of time. A quick thought came to my mind—almost like the thought did that day I was driving by the river—that I should get our handheld revolver and shoot myself. It was such a short and fleeting thought—I quickly pushed it out of my mind—but it had come. And as I sat on the floor crying my eyes out, I reminded myself that God still loved me in the midst of everything. And I reminded myself that I had so much to live for. All of those bad things may have happened, but I didn't really want to die; in fact, I knew I loved life way too much. I just wanted the pain to end. As I gathered my resolve as I'd had to do so many times before over the last year, I told myself that somehow all of this was going to work out.

+ + +

After we'd received all of the news about what caused our son to pass away, I started thinking of ways we could continue to be a blessing to others. Some of the moms I had talked to right after our son passed away told me the holidays could be rough. So I started thinking of ways I could help other families who had lost children as we approached the holidays. I was thinking that maybe we could have an ornament party so we could get together and honor our children.

In the months since Junior's passing, I sadly learned that four of the nearly twenty women I knew from work or church who had been pregnant with me had also suffered the loss of the children they were carrying. As I started doing more research on how many women experience the death of a child, I learned that the statistic is pretty high. One in four women experiences some sort of pregnancy loss or infant death over the course of her lifetime. As startling as that was for me to learn, I was curious as to why people didn't talk about it much. That statistic meant I definitely wasn't by myself on this journey, and I knew I wanted to do something to help other families know they weren't alone either.

I'd mentioned the ornament party idea to one of my friends who had also lost her son a couple of years prior, and to my surprise, as soon as I mentioned it, she said, "Let's do it!" Her agreement that I should do it was all I needed to get the ball rolling. After she and I talked some more, we started to think that maybe our ornament party shouldn't be a one-time event. That maybe it should be something more official, something where people met once every other month. I wanted to bring legitimacy to whatever we were doing, so I wanted to connect with medical professionals, psychologists, and community workers and get them involved in whatever this was that we were putting together. I scheduled a meeting with a bereavement coordinator so I could gain some additional insight into what types of information would be good to present at our first meeting. As I was driving to meet the bereavement coordinator, the name Angel Baby Network came to me. It stuck with me and I liked the name of it. We would be a network of parents, professionals, and supporters who were gathering to honor our angel babies.

When I met with the bereavement coordinator that day, I shared the name with her. She liked it, and I told her with a smile that I did too.

So, in December, four and half months after our little boy passed away, Angel Baby Network was launched. We've had people of different races, different religions, and different economic statuses with different stories come to our meetings. We've had psychologists, medical professionals, and community workers come and share information about their services with our families so that, if needed, they could get additional help. We've hosted events such as a butterfly release to honor our children's lives, and we participated in an international flag day that honors children who have passed away. Our story has been shared in publications online, in print, and on television, and we know that we are just getting started.

To reflect on it all has been amazing. Some people spend a lifetime never discovering their purpose. But within ten short days, our little boy came to this earth, figured it out, and left, charging his parents to carry out his purpose of bringing healing to bereaved families.

I've come to learn that child loss is something that brings people together in a unique way. There is an unexplainable connection that exists among bereaved parents. Unless someone has experienced it, he or she will never know what it feels like. I refer to us as the sorority and fraternity that no one wants to be a part of, because although none of us would ever wish to lose our child or children, there is an instant connection when two people find out they have done so.

Child loss is something that hurts deeply, but Chris and I, my parents, his parents, and so many other families around the world are proof that, as unbearable as it may seem, life will go on. I once described it on the Angel Baby Network website in a blog titled, "The Raw Truth about Infant and Child Loss."

The Raw Truth about Infant and Child Loss

Warning: This post contains a couple of bad words. If you have never endured the passing away of your child, you shouldn't have anything to say about those words. But if you are a parent who has lost a child, you will be able to identify.

I had once heard that there is nothing like losing a child. And until it happened to me, I couldn't fully comprehend the idea. I didn't understand how or why there was "nothing like losing a child," but based off of what I'd heard, I knew that it was something I never wanted to go through. I also didn't think it was something I'd ever know how to live through.

And then it happened to me.

*On Friday, July 31, at 7:23 p.m., in one of the NICU private rooms—room B7 to be exact—with our baby boy in my arms, his daddy/my husband looking over my shoulder and crying and tears flowing down my face, I learned that there is nothing like losing a child. *God, please don't let there be anything worse than losing a child.**

There is no hurt so deep, no pain so devastating, no circumstance so terrible that compares to it. I'm talking past your surface, through your flesh, into your muscles, on into your bones and beyond into your marrow... hurt. Your feelings' feelings hurt, and there is no one or nothing that is able to console you enough.

And when that pain doesn't fully manifest, there are times when you will be numb. Shell-shocked. Frozen in your state of mind, body, and the depths of your psychosocial soul over whatever the hell just happened—because you and everyone around you is still trying to make sense of it when it simply doesn't make sense.

It is a shitty situation. It is a fucked-up situation. It is a situation that will leave you asking God and people a million questions that no one will have the answer to. The most frequent and elusive question of them all will be, "WHY?" Especially when you did nothing to cause your child's death.

Some days you will be fine. And other days you will be a complete and total wreck because you will face the reality that your child isn't here on earth with you. Some days you will experience a trigger that will cause you to face the fact that your child has passed away. But until it happens, you won't know that thing, person, place, smell, or sound is a trigger, and the tears will unexpectedly fall.

For example, as a little girl I rode the school bus every day. Normally, there is no fear in riding the school bus or driving behind a school bus. But now I know that if I leave for work at 8:32 in the morning that I am going to be behind a school bus that makes three stops to pick up children before it makes a turn and is out of my sight. And if I am thinking about my child at 8:32 in the morning and I am behind the school bus as it makes those three stops, I may blink a few times and find tears rolling down my face. It's because at that moment I realize that my baby isn't on that school bus, and the harsh truth is he isn't ever going to ride on a school bus. And that hurts.

The raw truth about infant and child loss is that while people mean well, sometimes they say really, really stupid things and you have to look at them, breathe deeply, roll your eyes, shake your head, and forgive them. You will have to be the bigger person and understand that they didn't know what else to say. And on that day, that person or those people forgot that a hug and an "I'm praying for you" would've gone a lot farther than a cliché phrase. You will have to take several deep breaths and sometimes explain to them that time doesn't heal all wounds, that none of your other children will replace the one that passed away, and that just because you're young, it doesn't necessarily mean that you are ready to get pregnant right away after your child has died.

The raw truth about infant and child loss is that as a parent whose infant or child has passed away, you will have bittersweet moments when your friends tell you that they are pregnant, and while you are so happy and elated for them, you will be sad because it isn't you. You may get sad at your friends' children graduating if your child was supposed to graduate at the same time. Or you may have to explain that you don't want an invite to their child's birthday party because it is too painful for you to attend, since you know your child should be celebrating a birthday at the same time.

As a parent, you will long for the everyday things that other parents take for granted. The good-bye kiss that they receive from their child as they drop them off for a sleepover at a friend's house. Staying up late with their child to help them with homework or a science fair. Hearing the pitter-patter of feet run through the house during the wee hours of a Saturday morning. The noise of giggling late at night when their child is supposed to be asleep. The phone call that their child makes to them or vice versa just to say hello. Even their child asking 100 annoying questions or begging for money are all things that you will desire just one more time that other parents take for granted.

But I also have to come to know that as a parent whose child now lives in heaven, that the truth about infant and child loss is that it can give you a completely different perspective on life…if you let it. You will come to realize that you possess a strength that allows you to get through life's most tumultuous of times. You will wake up in the morning, put on your imaginary superhero cape and make it one more day, which turns into tomorrow and the day after that.

If you let it, infant and child loss can lead you to love more deeply. It will cause you to forget about things that aren't really important. It will remind you of what really matters. It will challenge you to truly live in the moment, because as a parent who has lost an infant or a child, you know all too well that the next moment isn't promised.

The raw truth about infant and child loss is that it sucks. It hurts…a lot. But it will connect you to what I like to call the sorority and fraternity that no one wants to be a part of. You will feel an instant connection to others who have walked a similar walk as you. You will meet and befriend some of the most amazing people who are just like you, who have experienced infant and child death, and who will hug you when you need it, check on you when you feel like you are falling apart, and will be silent as they sit with you while you cry on those very hard days.

As you endure infant and child loss, at times you will truly begin to understand that as you walk this road, Philippians 4:7 will leap off of the pages of the Bible and become true. "And the peace of God which surpasses ALL understanding will keep your hearts and minds in Christ Jesus." You will come to know a peace that you didn't even know you could experience.

Infant and child loss isn't easy…but if you make the commitment to getting up one more day and to continue living on this earth with your child living in heaven—but always in your heart—it is doable. Hang in there. You are stronger than you know.

+ + +

Chris and I make it a point to talk about our son and to listen to each other when we start thinking about how our lives would've been had he lived. Chris always laughs and jokes about how he wishes Junior had lived so that Junior could get in trouble with him. And when I see some of the other babies who were born around the same time that he was, I get nostalgic and think about what my baby would look like and what he would be doing.

Two of the hardest days for me to deal with since our son passed away were New Year's Eve and the anniversary of our baby shower. When everyone else was saying good-bye to the former year and going into the new year, I felt like I couldn't join in. The year that our son was born and died was a defining year for Chris and me. And we don't get to leave it in the past. And my baby shower was one of the most heartfelt celebrations I'd ever experienced. The joy and the sadness I felt on its anniversary date was a lot to bear.

Chris and I have continued to go through tests, trials, twists, and turns. The symptoms of MS aren't the most friendly in the world, but Chris continues to courageously fight that battle every single day, and he has me by his side to do it. We eventually learned that some of the symptoms were slowing him down and preventing him from doing the same type of work he was so used to doing before we got married. After several temporary work contracts ended, we were able to get Chris involved in a program that helps people who have been diagnosed with disabilities by connecting those people with jobs and resources that will help them on a long-term basis. When MS symptoms show up, Chris's determination and perseverance show up even stronger.

Exactly a year after our son passed away, we were planning to move into a house that we would rent and then own, but twelve days before we were supposed to move, the house caught on fire. We ended up enduring a traumatic move in which the movers we hired swindled us out of money, damaged our property, and left most of our belongings outside the building we were moving into. But once again, our family and friends came to our assistance and helped us get on our feet. And as if we needed more excitement, during that same month, a person hit Chris in a hit-and-run accident and totaled his car.

We've been asked how we've been able to maintain our strength through our circumstances. We have three simple answers. One, we have a relationship with God, individually and collectively. We know Him and He knows us. And us knowing Him is bigger than a church membership or basing our faith on what someone else has experienced. Two, we always knew we wanted our son's life to have a great purpose. That didn't stop when he died, and it didn't stop *because* he died. And three, we don't have a choice other than to be strong. We are fighters who fight to win every single time. We are like the old-school knock-out dolls. A person can knock one of those dolls down, but it always bounces back up because it is made with weights at the bottom of it—and it is determined not to stay down. God is our foundation, and He grounds us so that no matter how many times we are knocked down, we will always get up.

In the midst of the trials, there are always silver linings. In September 2016, I was recognized as one of the distinctive "Forty Young Professionals Under the Age of 40" in our region for the contributions I'd made to my city and community, on a professional and personal level. And in the same month, I was able to travel to Columbus, Ohio, to testify in front of our State Senate's Health and Human Services Committee on behalf of a bill that was written specifically to reduce infant mortality across our state. I found out the next day that the bill had passed through to the House. In January 2017, Ohio Governor John Kasich signed the bill into law.

At the encouragement of my husband, I enrolled in modeling and acting classes, and I can't wait to see what successes that brings.

At the end of the day, Chris and I were two young people who got married on the premise that we loved God and we loved each other. Before we got married, the image in our heads was that of walks in the park every day and nothing but smiles. But we've learned that there's more than that to marriage. It already takes a lot of work and commitment, and when hard times happen, it takes a lot of extra love and patience, too.

We vowed to stay together for better or worse. It doesn't get much worse than losing a child. At least I pray it doesn't. We said we would stay together through richer and poorer. We have had much money, and we have been sued over money that we did not have. We promised we would stay together in sickness and in health. We've both dealt with medical diagnoses. We are two people who simply made commitments, and we have stuck to them. And even though some people shy away from psychological and marital counseling, it has helped us through our situations immensely. There are times when we get frustrated with each other and frustrated with life in general. But we also laugh every day. We know we have many more years to go, and we know there will be more surprises ahead. But as long as we've got each other on earth, Junior in our hearts, and we continue to stand on our faith in God and in His Word, we will be fine.

We find joy in focusing on the current day. Just as Matthew 6:34 reads: "Give your entire attention to what God is doing right now, and don't get worked up about what may or may not happen tomorrow. God will help you deal with whatever hard things come up when the time comes."

We may not know what tomorrow holds, but we know Who holds tomorrow. And that is enough for us.

ACKNOWLEDGMENTS

We want to give an extra special thanks to the Lewis and Jones families, who have shown us unconditional and unyielding love. Thank you for being there for us. Thank you for reminding us that no matter what, God was still watching over us. Every time you sat with us, cried with us, laughed with us, made dinner for us, let us just be us, prayed for us, and told us it would be okay, plus everything else you have done for us, has mattered and has touched us deeply. We have been able to soar because you are the wind beneath our wings. Thank you to our friends, extended family members, coworkers, and church families who have shown us God's love in action. Thank you for your acts of kindness and for checking on us to make sure we were okay when you knew times were hard for us. We also want to thank the seven couples who specifically prayed for us every day of the week as we waited on God to perform a miracle. It may look different than we thought it would, but God definitely answered our prayers and gave us a miracle.

Thank you to our Angel Baby Network family. You mean more to us than you will ever know. You give us life. Thank you for your honesty, for living your truth, and for reminding us we are not alone. How special we must be for our children to have brought us together.

Thank you to our doctors who took the best care of us and of our son. Thank you for allowing us to believe the best for our child even if your medical knowledge leaned toward a different outcome. We appreciate you for hoping with us.

And finally, we want to acknowledge all of the bereaved parents around the world. You are not alone. The author of the quote may be anonymous, but we know the words are true: "Child loss is not an event. It is an indescribable journey of survival." Keep on surviving and continue to keep your child's memory alive.

Here are a few Bible verses that have special meaning for us and have helped us stay strong through everything we've faced together. We hope you'll hold them in your heart, as well!

"Faith is the substance of things hoped for, the evidence of things unseen."

—Hebrews 11:1

"For I know the plans I have for you, declares the Lord, plans to prosper you and not to harm you, plans to give you hope and a future."

—Jeremiah 29:11

"And we know that all things work together for good to them that love God, to them who are called according to His purpose."

—Romans 8:28

"But He said to me, 'My grace is sufficient for you, for my power is made perfect in weakness.'"

—2 Corinthians 12:9

"Therefore take up the whole armor of God, that you may be able to withstand…and having done all, to stand firm."

—Ephesians 6:13

"…Weeping may last through the night, but joy comes with the morning."

—Psalms 30:5

ABOUT THE ANGEL BABY NETWORK

AngelBabyNetwork.org

History

In July 2015, Christopher Jones Sr. and Danielle Jones had their first child, Christopher Jones Jr. Christopher Jr., also referred to as "Junior," was born with multiple congenital abnormalities due to a genetic defect. At ten days old, his short life on earth ended, but his purpose was only beginning. Out of a desire to help other parents who had suffered pregnancy or infant loss, Danielle and a friend whose son was born still started the Angel Baby Network.

Mission

Our mission is to help parents who have endured a pregnancy and/or infant loss and to give them a hand to hold as they walk through such a devastating time in their lives.

Vision

Our ultimate vision is to connect parents, social services workers, medical professionals, and licensed psychologists from across the country to one another as bereaved parents walk through the death of their child.

Purpose

We exist to ensure that parents do not go through the death of their child alone, by offering resources so they can get the help they need and social gatherings so they can connect with other parents who can identify with their circumstance.

How Does It Work?

By connecting with birthing hospitals, maternal fetal medicine high-risk clinics, and children's hospitals, the Angel Baby Network will serve as a peer-to-peer group to which parents who have lost a child can be referred. If desired, a person or couple who has lost a child will be referred to a person or couple who is already a part of the Angel Baby Network and who is at least six months beyond child loss. That Angel Baby Network member will be the "buddy" to the new parent or parents. In addition to this, the Angel Baby Network will meet once every other month to engage its members in a relaxed, fun social activity where they will meet and can identify with one another. At each gathering, a licensed psychologist will be present in case a person or a couple needs information about additional mental health and emotional support. Information about local social services agencies and other local support groups that help parents who experience the loss of a child also will be available.

Information and Statistics on Infant Mortality

Infant mortality rate is used by demographers to measure the number of infants who die before their first birthday for every one thousand births in a given year. Measures of infant mortality are among the best indicators of general health conditions in a population and are often used to estimate overall morbidity and death rates in countries with incomplete vital statistics records. According to the Centers for Disease Control and Prevention website, *www.cdc.gov:*

> More than 23,000 infants died in the United States in 2013. The loss of a baby remains a sad reality for many families and takes a serious toll on the health and well-being of families, as well as the nation.
>
> For every 1,000 babies that are born, six die during their first year. Most of these babies die as a result of:

- Birth defects
- Preterm birth (birth before thirty-seven weeks' gestation) and low birth weight
- Sudden Infant Death Syndrome (SIDS)
- Maternal complications in childbirth
- Injuries (e.g., suffocation)

These five causes of infant mortality together accounted for about 57 percent of all infant deaths in the United States in 2013.

ABOUT THE AUTHORS

Christopher and Danielle Jones are a fun-loving couple who make sure to laugh every day. They have weathered a variety of storms throughout their lives, all while holding on to their faith in God and their love for each other. Chris is a graduate of the University of Cincinnati, where he earned a bachelor's degree in marketing and an associate's degree in business. He has turned his photography hobby into a business, at joneseight.com. Danielle is a graduate of Florida A&M University, where she earned a degree in public relations, and the University of Cincinnati, where she earned her MBA. Chris and Danielle are passionate about supporting families who have endured child loss, and they seek to inspire others with their story of loss and love.